O F    T H E    M I N D

# Odyssey of the Mind

*A Voyage of Discovery*

Eugene T. Woolf

*Sculptures by Jerry Anderson*

SOUTHERN UTAH UNIVERSITY PRESS
CEDAR CITY, UTAH

Library of Congress Catalog Card Number: 97-66546

ISBN Number: 0-935615-11-3

Printed in the United States of America

10   9   8   7   6   5   4   3   2   1

UTAH
**DESERT RAT**
LES MISCH
2884 S Rim Rock Lane, Moab, UT 84532

# CONTENTS

# THE AUTHOR:

## *Eugene T. Woolf*

*E*ugene T. Woolf is Professor Emeritus of Philosophy and Literature and Director of the Grace Adams Tanner Center for Human Values at Southern Utah University. He received his degrees from the University of Utah and did doctoral work at Stanford University. He also studied at Shrivenham University in England. In his 44 years of service to SUU, he has occupied a number of administrative positions, including Chair of the English Department, Dean of the College of Arts and Letters, and Administrative Assistant to the President. He has evaluated academic programs at several Utah colleges and universities for the Utah State Office of Education and for the State Board of Regents. For several years he held the position of Associate Commissioner for Academic Affairs in the Utah System of Higher Education. Dr. Woolf served as President of the Utah Council of Teachers of English, which presented him with a "Lifetime Achievement Award"; Chair of the Utah Humanities Council; and President of the Iron County School Board. He was a member of the board of directors of the Utah Shakespearean Festival for fifteen years, and for several years was a member of the National Board of Advisors of the Institute for Advanced Philosophic Research. Dr. Woolf has been invited to address numerous social and professional organizations and has participated in state and national meetings regarding a variety of academic subjects. He has served as a consultant to the National Council of Teachers of English, the New Jersey Educational Bank, and to industry and government. Dr. Woolf has prepared texts for his courses in philosophy for the last several years, and is the author of articles on Henry James, Herman Melville, Theodore Winthrop, and on social political and educational philosophy. He is the author of a book about the life and writings of Theodore Winthrop.

# THE SCULPTOR:

# *Jerry Anderson*

Jerry Anderson is a noted Utah sculptor who resides in Silver Reef (Leeds), Utah, where he has maintained his studio. Born in Las Vegas, Nevada, in 1935, he is the son of a well driller. The family moved to Manti, Utah, when Anderson was six years old. His father drilled wells in almost every town in Utah, often involving his sons in his business. Unable to finish high school because of their work schedule, the three Anderson sons received their high school diplomas by correspondence through American Schools in Chicago, Illinois. He married his wife, Fawn Olsen, in 1954. Upon the death of his father, Anderson and his wife moved to southern California, where he worked for a steel fabrication company. At this time, too, Anderson enrolled in the famous artist correspondence course which taught commercial flat work art as well as anatomy of all living things. It took four years to complete the course, Anderson working eight hours at a regular job then studying well into the night. For 26 years, however, Anderson pursued a career in the steel business while his artist skills languished. Finally in 1981 he left the steel industry to devote the remainder of his life to sculpting. Highly gifted, he has become widely recognized as a master of bronze sculpture, his works characterized by strong design and careful attention to anatomy and historical detail. By 1997, he had created 70 small size, limited edition bronzes, 15 of them on the campus of Southern Utah University. His work can be found in many private and museum collections from California to Washington D.C. His sculptures have twice won the "Best of Show" award at the American-Canadian Classic exhibition; and he has been featured in news articles and television newscasts throughout the American West as a sculptor of uncommon power and skill.

# *Preface*

The chapters in this book appeared originally as separate articles published in the Southern Utah University *Journal*. They were issued over a period of twelve months in connection with the unveiling of the statues of the twelve men and women which comprise the Centurium, the university's centennial gift to the twenty-first century.

The Centurium is the "brain child" of Dr. Gerald R. Sherratt, president of the university. He has taken responsibility for seeing to the design and execution of every phase of the project, and was instrumental in arranging for individual and corporate sponsors of the statues, without whose financial support this project could not have been realized. President Sherratt, with the help of Mr. Stuart Jones and his competent staff, has raised the funds needed to cover the entire costs connected with the Centurium.

In an effort to recognize the role of academic excellence that is central to every higher education institution, President Sherratt requested my assistance in selecting twelve historical figures from Western civilization who were among those who had the greatest impact upon the course of history through their impressive display of human thought.

To bring these figures to life, President Sherratt selected Mr. Jerry Anderson, a remarkably talented sculptor, whose work has appeared in exhibits in the United States from coast to coast. I have in the course of the past twelve months developed a close relationship with Mr. Anderson. I have visited his home and studio in Leeds, Utah, where I have witnessed the figures emerging from steel and clay. Mr. Anderson's work displays a remarkable anatomical correctness which is matched by the appropriateness of pose and the felicity of expression of the men and women, whom, through his genius, he has brought to life. Despite its western orientation, his work reveals an incredible level of sophistication, which manifests itself in the work of every great artist. It is his ability to transcend time, place, and circumstance that has won him praise and awards in many sections of the United States.

To help with the designing of period clothing of the figures proposed for the Centurium, Mr. Anderson enlisted the aid of Mrs. Olive Esplin, who served as his historical researcher and costume designer. An instructor emeritus at Dixie College, Mrs. Esplin has had more than twenty years' experience designing and constructing costumes for more than one hundred theatrical productions. Her fastidious attention to detail is apparent in the clothes she has designed for the figures of the Centurium.

In the preparation of my text, I have consulted hundreds of sources from my own library, the university library, and by way of inter-library loans. I have found my source material to be both fascinating and frustrating, but never intimidating. Rather than attempt an originality that was elusive, I have helped myself to the banquet prepared by my literary hosts, who, in every instance, have helped themselves to the fruits of their predecessors. I am, therefore, in the preparation of this text, not so much a generator of ideas as I am an historian of them. From the pages of the countless authors who have assembled a marvelous wealth of detail regarding the lives of my twelve luminaries, I have selected material which, in my judgment, gives a balanced perspective. Much of the material in these pages is taken piecemeal from my source material; and, when appropriate to the tenor of my work, I have often helped myself to the felicitous phrases of my sources, finding no better method of revealing the colorful character of the subject matter. When required, I have quoted my sources, or made reference to them by name.

I must acknowledge the assistance I have received from others in the preparation of this work. I am grateful to Professors S.S. Moorty and Steven Heath for their careful reading of my manuscripts, and to President Gerald R. Sherratt for making me listen while he read each manuscript aloud.

I am especially indebted to my secretary, Ronda Gardner, without whose help this project could not have been completed in the time allotted to it. The personal interest she took in the preparation of the manuscripts went beyond anything I could have reasonably expected of her.

Finally, I acknowledge the unfailing support of my wife, Leslie, the first reader of my articles, whose uncommon common sense had helped to keep me focused and has kept this work half its intended length.

Eugene T. Woolf
Southern Utah University
January 4, 1997

# *Introduction*

In selecting the twelve men and women from history who have earned the label "great," I recognize that all sorts of value judgments are involved. While someone may be called 'great' because he or she has significant value for a specific population or community, it is usually considered safer for one to use the term to apply to those who, by general consensus, have exerted a significant influence on successive generations. In this context it is intended that great men and women are those who have made important contributions in the development of Western values, with respect to their propagation, their analyses, and their preservation.

But why, it may be asked, have I not included figures from the East as well as from the West, or why have I not included highly visible minority figures? I can only reply that, regarding the second part of the question, we are all minorities, judged from one perspective or another; besides, the men and women were chosen for specific attributes, not because they were generally representative, or had great popular appeal. The first part of the question deserves a fuller answer. The wisdom of the East is as deserving of attention as that of the West, to be sure, but other considerations come into play. I could not have included Eastern figures without diluting the concentration I have attempted in this project. While it is true that the two cultures are showing a remarkable ability to close the gap that has traditionally separated them, it is also true that Western thought is still largely self-contained, making possible a special treatment of it. It is, moreover, a commonly recognized fact that the scientific and philosophic tradition of the West exhibits speculations and methods quite different from those employed by the Eastern mind. Only in the Greek civilization, as my article on Socrates suggests, does philosophy go hand in hand with science; and it was the ability to meld science and philosophy which gave the civilization of the West its character.

It has been wittily observed that science and philosophy were born precisely at the same time—on May 28 at 6:30 p.m, 585 BC. (Melesian Standard Time). Behind this witticism lies the physical fact that a solar eclipse began at that time in the city of Miletus on the Ionian Coast. The Greek philosopher Thales predicted the eclipse, though perhaps not the exact time of it. The important thing in all this, it has been suggested, is not how close Thales came in his prediction. It took modern astronomers to establish the exact date. What is important is that Thales could even make a prediction, thus recognizing the existence of natural law. At this point science and philosophy were undistinguishable. But, more than that, something new had been added to the way the universe was viewed, and it took the ancient Greeks to provide that.

In undertaking a project such as this, I cannot avoid presenting a certain amount of biographical data; but this book is not a series of biographical sketches in the traditional sense of chronologically recounting events in the lives of individual men and women. It is, rather, a look at the intellectual context in which those lives were lived.

In short, my treatment of material is contextual rather than linear. It attempts to define and place in perspective certain features of my subjects—their attitudes, their influence on others, or others' influence on them, their motivation, their very human characters.

I have chosen to present the figures in chronological order by group heading. To the extent this work can be called a history, it is an intellectual history.

My purpose has been to present the subjects of my studies in as balanced a manner as possible. This has been a difficult task because of the diversity of opinion of my sources regarding these twelve men and women. What originality I claim is in the selection of material which, in my judgment, gives the most generally accepted assessment regarding the life and thought of each person under consideration. I have made an honest attempt to refrain from interjecting my personal opinion into matters being discussed; but it was, of course, impossible to do so. What personal observations I have allowed myself have been prompted by fifty years' experience as a graduate student and as a teacher of the humanities. I make no apologies for my own biases. They have been honestly and laboriously arrived at.

I have not sought in my distillations of the legacy of these heroes of history to offer more than history itself allows. A review of only a portion of the great body of literature available to me has revealed many contradictory points of view which I have not attempted to resolve. What I have attempted is to suggest to the reader the element of genius residing in each of these figures represented in the

Centurium in order that there might emerge a sense of their worthiness to be captured in bronze.

Thus the selection of figures represented in the Centurium has been neither arbitrary nor superficial. Any attempt to capture the essence of the great minds of Western civilization which have made an enduring impact because of the timeless nature of their expressions will at best result in charges of bias and at worst in charges of ignorance. Of course I plead guilty to both. Every thoughtful person has his or her own list of preferred figures of history, and hardly two people would submit identical lists; and I freely acknowledge that other remarkable figures of history are as worthy for having tribute paid them as those I have selected. But there is method in my madness, which goes beyond the fact that each of the persons selected for the Centurium is eminently worthy of the honor.

The selection of categories under which to gather the figures contained in them is a natural matching of character to category. The "Exaltation of Reason," the "Fire of Genius," the "Passion for Freedom," and the "Spirit of Discovery" are fortuitous expressions of the Odyssey of the Mind, and they attract candidates in a remarkably logical way.

But why did I select three Greek philosophers from the Hellenic Age of Athens, belonging to successive generations, to represent the "Exaltation of Reason"? Surely other men and women in the annals of Western civilization cared as much about "reason" as they. Perhaps, but Western civilization is what it is in a large measure because Socrates, Plato, and Aristotle were the first to glorify reason, and they laid the foundation of intellectual thought for the entire Western world. Building on one another's strength, they individually and collectively delivered some of the finest and most enduring expressions of the human mind. In doing so, they set the course that Western civilization was to follow. Together they constitute the very bedrock of the Western mind. In many real and tangible ways, we have failed to outgrow or outdo them.

It is not so much that Socrates, Plato, and Aristotle themselves exalted reason. It is that, in promoting it so powerfully and sublimely, they have inspired and instructed generations of those who, like them, loved wisdom. The world may little note nor long remember what they *did* there, but it can never forget what they *said* there.

The figures selected for the 'Fire of Genius' include Leonardo da Vinci, William Shakespeare, and Marie Curie. What they demonstrated was a passion for the ideas that ruled their lives. But what they also demonstrated was a keen sense of the value of human emotions. Their ability to render the world around them as an emotional experience, and their own contributions in helping to enlarge that emotional experience, is especially noteworthy. Each would have found favor with the remark King Arthur is made to offer in *Camelot*: "What good is reason if it doesn't touch the heart?" The figures of the "Fire of Genius" are usually represented as cerebral in everything they undertook, but such a description fails to account for the part that their emotions played in informing their intellects. While Galileo, Newton, and Einstein had no need to refer to observable data to justify their thoughts, da Vinci, Shakespeare, and Curie all required the materials of their art—da Vinci the media of his art, Shakespeare the English language, and Curie her test tube and labaratory—and their emotional attachment to these materials is incontestable.

The defenders of political and intellectual freedom all lived within a hundred years of each other. They are listed under "The Passion for Freedom." All three inhabited a world in which democracy had taken on the mantle of respectability. But it was not so well entrenched that liberty was considered to be an indispensable ingredient of it. In fact, so tenuous was the concept of liberty that those opposed to it were as vocal as they were numerous. In the case of Thomas Jefferson, Germaine de Staël, and John Stuart Mill, the recognition of personal liberty—intellectual as well as political—was grounded in the belief that men and women in all countries made better citizens when the authority of the state was limited to what public order and efficiency demanded. These defenders of freedom believed that while social order may be an excuse for limiting freedom, efficiency was not.

The category titled "the Spirit of Discovery" contains another trio whose names are inextricably linked. In their case, however, a period of three hundred years separate them. They departed radically from the views of nature held by the Greeks, and, as a result, they provide a whole new perspective from which to view the universe.

What Galileo Galilei, Isaac Newton, and

Albert Einstein provided was an uncanny ability to marry hypothesis to mathematics. All of them thought that their hypotheses did not require demonstration. They were intuitively correct, and their mathematical formulae were simply illustrations of their theories. But in method and in character they were unique. They did, however, understand the value of observation and experimentation in science, and they demonstrated competency in applying them.

To find value in an undertaking such as this, one has to believe that one's mind can actually be shaped by the supreme intellectual gifts of those who have preceded us. Ideas, like blood, intermingle. Our ideas are all in some measure dependent upon the thought of others; but, as Socrates pointed out 2,400 years ago, we are capable of limitless learning. My focus had been on the role of the intellect in bringing about and sustaining those values, and on the ultimate supremacy of the life of the mind.

However unsubstantial and tenuous the thread of civilization may be, man's future is not necessarily controlled by the past. We are as much affected by ideas as by events, and the direction that cultures take—even whole civilizations—often derives from a single thought. No study of the great events of history could ignore the ideas from which they sprung.

Any significant change which takes place can be measured by the effect it has on our own mental processes. This study of how men and women who have expressed in a remarkable and indelible way their commitment to the life of the mind, will reveal that history has a logical as well as a chronological structure, and that ideas as well as events reveal the story of our progress and our growth.

The Centurium serves to capture the odyssey of the mind through twenty-five centuries of Western civilization. But this story of the mind is limited to ideas which have significantly affected the course of history. Thus the Centurium may be described as the embodiment of the intellect in bronze.

I tend to view these figures as men and women standing in a room carrying on a great conversation. A banquet of ideas is spread before them, but it is a movable feast, an inexhaustible feast which lies before them and before all of us; and we are invited to participate in the conversation.

We come full circle in a sense—no pun is intended, but it can hardly be avoided—moving from Socrates to Einstein, who are kindred spirits.

But then, perhaps, by now we should have learned that we are all kindred spirits. What we have in common is our humanity. It is only when we leave our narrow rooms and look beyond the smoke of our own chimneys that we can see the depth and breadth of that humanity. That is the ultimate lesson of the intellect, and it is reflected in the motto of Southern Utah University: "Learning lives forever."

SOCRATES

BY
JERRY
ANDERSON

# Socrates
## 469-399 BC

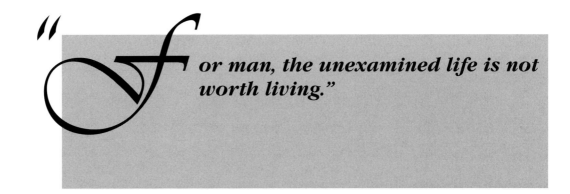

"*For man, the unexamined life is not worth living.*"

Almost twenty-four hundred years have passed since Socrates, sentenced to death by his fellow citizens, drank the cup of hemlock at the prison in Athens. Few events have resulted in such a remarkable change in the way people looked at the content of their minds and at the way they lived their lives. The only event which can be compared to it is the crucifixion of Christ some four hundred years later. Thus, it was well said, "The world never quite forgot the message that was left on that spring day in 399 BC."

So what was the message? Socrates left nothing, really—no school, no disciples (by his own account), no system of thought, no writings, no solution to the countless questions he raised. Like Christ, he was "called" to be a prophet; like Christ, his conduct in public life made the authorities sufficiently uneasy to put him to death. As a result, Socrates became the first martyr of any prominence in the cause of philosophy.

Socrates did not invent philosophy, but he gave it its most respected interpretation. And he did not invent the soul, but he gave it its most enduring interpretation: Philosophy is associated with Socrates in its purest form, free from dogmatism of every kind. The soul received from Socrates the first moral account of it in all Western thought.

Almost every serious discussion of Socrates starts with what is called the "Socratic problem"—the question of the reliability of the sources which treat of the life and character of Socrates of Athens. The sources are few, and some are hostile. Only one exists that made reference to him while he was still alive, and that is *The Clouds* by the comic playwright Aristophanes in 423 BC. Both Plato and Xenophon, though much younger, attached themselves to Socrates and knew him personally. Aeschines, who was about the same age as Plato and Xenophon, also wrote about Socrates, but his testimony is considered less reliable. Plato combines his veneration for Socrates, his considerable talent as a poet, and his own great insight as a philosopher, to present an account of Socrates which has earned them both enduring fame.

Of course, to refer to Plato as the primary biographer of Socrates is to beg the question. Did Socrates actually exist or was he only a figment of a variety of excited imaginations? The question is not frivolous in light of the fact that about the only incontestable thing about Socrates is the event of his death in 399 BC.

While Plato's judgment may be loaded with a superabundance of idealism, it is he who has presented the Socrates the world thinks it knows. On Plato's side is the fact that he wrote the material dealing with Socrates' life, thought, and death, knowing that it would be read by the very men who attended Socrates during the month he waited for the death sentence to be carried out; and it seems highly unlikely that he would fabricate a story that would offend those who, like Crito, knew and befriended Socrates during his entire life. Plato tells the story of Socrates' trial, imprisonment, and execution in three short dialogues—*Apology, Crito,* and *Phaedo.*

The date of Socrates' death is a matter of official record. A Register of Archons based on the ancient records lists that date as the archonship of Laches, 400/399 BC. His execution was delayed for a month because the trial started the day after the beginning of the Delian festival, during which no executions were permitted. Since that festival took place during the spring, scholars trace the time of his birth back at least seventy archonships, to 470 or 469, on the strength of Plato's testimony that Socrates was seventy or more at the time of his trial.

The seventy years of Socrates' life encompassed the most glorious years Athens ever experienced, and no other place has witnessed anything like it, before or since. The intellectual and artistic accomplishments of the Periclean Age were stimulated by the Athenian victory over the Persians in 479 BC. In a period of ten years, the Athenians had twice turned aside the invading Persian army and navy, and the ideal of liberty took on special importance. In the span of just fifty years, Athens was to emerge as the foremost of the numerous Greek city-states. And, during that time, Socrates would have seen the new Parthenon rise on the Acropolis in its incredible splendor. He would have watched the first performances of the great Greek tragedies, and he would have come under the influence of some of the greatest thinkers in the history of human thought. From the Athenians' defeat of the Persians to the beginning of the Peloponnesian War—the fifty-year period from 480 to 431—there occurred in Athens an unparalled energy of mind and body, a versatility of thinking, a clarity of expression, and an explosive intelligence that would, from that time of ours, characterize "the glory that was Greece."

Athens by today's standards was a small city of scarcely more than some hundred thousand inhabitants living in an area of under a thousand square miles. The city was divided into political units called "demes," from which democracy takes its name. Socrates belonged to the deme of Alopeké and the tribe of Antiochid, as did Crito, a gifted and wealthy man who remained a friend of Socrates for his entire life.

Socrates' father was reported to have been a stone carver or sculptor, and his mother a midwife, a profession practiced by people of advanced social standing. Of Socrates' profession, if he had one, there is no record. Some scholars have suggested that, like his father, he was a sculptor, but that theory is now largely discredited. It has been suggested that Socrates may have married a woman who died before she could bear him children. More certain is the record that late in life he married a woman much younger than he named Xanthippe, and that he had three sons by her. (At the time of Socrates' death at age seventy, the oldest boy was about seventeen. The youngest was still carried in his mother's arms.)

While still very young, Socrates received the usual "elementary" education of his day, which included gymnastics and music. "Secondary" education was provided by the elders of the deme and family, and it included the proper observance of religious deities and political responsibilities. Socrates is reported to have developed an early interest in geometry and astronomy.

His family was by all accounts well connected. His father is said to have been a friend of Aristides the Just, and Socrates himself belonged to the circle of Pericles.

Socrates had extensive service in the Athenian army. He earned a reputation for stamina and bravery during the years of his participation in the Peloponnesian War (c. 431-421), although the war dragged on until 404. At Potidaea (431) he saved the life of Alcibiades; and he served with distinction during the campaigns at Delium (424) and Amphipolis (422). One of the most compelling views of his hardiness was his habit of going barefoot into battle, even during the cold and snow of winter.

Adding to the eccentric behavior was his appearance, which was little short of grotesque. Stout and of medium height, he had bulging eyes, a wide mouth, a snub nose, and broad nostrils. But to all his friends, despite his look of Silenus or a Satyr, he was "all glorious within," displaying always good humor, cordiality, and remarkable charm. He was reduced to poverty by the war, ostensibly because of not being able to look after his personal affairs over such a long period of time. As a result he wore the same homespun clothing all year long. It was maintained that he appeared as indifferent to luxury as he was to suffering, and did not seek out even ordinary comforts. While generally avoiding strong drinks, he could, at a party, outdrink everyone and remain standing, apparently unaffected by alcohol. He spent his life in public—in the gymnasium, the lecture hall, or in a private home.

Even before the Peloponnesian War, Socrates had earned a reputation as a remarkable intellect, attracting to himself not only a large number of Athenian citizens, but foreigners from distant cities. One of his most enthusiastic disciples was the Athenian Chaerepho. It was Chaerepho who inquired of the oracle of Delphi whether anyone was wiser than Socrates. According to the oracle, no one was wiser, an answer that is said to have launched Socrates on the mission that would consume the remainder of his life and establish him as the founder of moral philosophy.

Now just what Socrates was renowned for before his mission call is not precisely known. In his early years he had passed through the phases of "passionate lover, religious mystic, eager rationalist, and humanist." Plato has Socrates referring to himself as a lifelong victim of Eros, and his erotic nature is the subject of much discussion; but, as A.E. Taylor points out, it would be a mistake to view that as incompatible with his "absolute moral purity."

Greek philosophy is centered on Socrates. It goes by the name of Pre-Socratic, Socratic, and Post-Socratic. Now why is Socrates considered the link in these movements? The answer provides interesting information about the nature of philosophy itself.

The ancient Greeks were not confined to the Attic Peninsula, but established colonies in Asia Minor and Southern Italy. It was in the city of Miletus, in what is now Turkey, that Greek philosophy began. The Pre-Socratic philosophers Thales, Anaximander, and Anaximenes were all citizens of Miletus. Because of the location of Miletus on the Ionian coast, their philosophy goes by the name of Ionian science. In their time—in the early sixth century BC—science and philosophy were inseparable. To say that the Greeks invented philosophy is to say that they invented science. It is well known that "philosophy" means the love of wisdom or skill, but it was not simply an application of reason. Science came into existence when Thales separated himself from the outside world and saw in nature forces that had nothing to do with himself as an individual. That, too, was the beginning of philosophy. Nature was for the first time held to be indifferent. And it was capable of being understood by the application of reason. The first assertions about nature were simple. Everything consisted of fire, or water, or earth, or air. Eventually experimentation followed speculation. Theory, which marked the focus of this early philosophy, was abandoned by many of the Pre-Socratics in favor of experiment and observation. In this way, science became distinct from philosophy and would occasionally conflict with it.

One of these Pre-Socratic philosophers, Anaxagoras, found his way to Athens about 480 BC and remained there for thirty years. He was thought to be a soldier in Xerxes' army, left in Athens after the war with Persia. His influence in Athens was exceptionally strong, and he became the friend and teacher of Pericles. Archelaus, the friend and teacher of Socrates, took over Anaxagoras' school after the latter's departure from Athens. And it has been suggested that Socrates eventually took over the school of Archelaus. So, it was Ionian science that first caught and held the enthusiasm of Socrates. But it held his interest only until an observation by Anaxagoras regarding an intelligent cause of the universe carried no meaning other than assigning it as first cause, or mover. Socrates demanded more than this. He demanded purpose.

The course of his life is said to have changed while he was still in the army. He is reported to have stood in a "rapt" for twenty-four hours, not moving nor speaking.

This extended "rapt" is not to be confused with the occasional fits of "rapt" for which Socrates was so well known. These were an expression of the "demon" or "divine sign" which Socrates had experienced since childhood. The sign manifested itself as a supernatural voice and served to prevent him from taking a particular harmful course of action, even about trivial matters. It was not a voice of conscience, and it seemed to have no particular bearing on matters of morality.

From the time of the curious "conversion" experienced in that extended "rapt," he devoted his life to testing the truth or the oracle—that no one was wiser than Socrates. How he went about this is well known. Professing ignorance (quite genuinely), he approached members of various classes of Athenian citizens, searching among them for someone wiser than he and finding none. The so-called "Socratic irony" is based on the

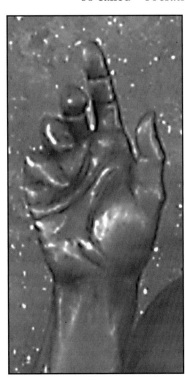

assumption that in his discussions he only pretended ignorance in order to catch his unsuspecting prey in his intellectual net, but that view hardly fits the description given by those who knew him best. The irony is more fittingly viewed as his being wise enough to be aware of his own lack of wisdom. It is not that the questions he asked were that difficult. He merely wanted those he engaged in conversation to explain how men should conduct their lives, how they should make their souls as good as possible. It was clear that Socrates had

turned his attention from the outward-looking stance of Ionian science to an inward-looking pattern of self-examination. On the temple of Apollo at Delphi could be read the inscription "Know thyself." It led Socrates to conclude that "for man, the unexamined life is not worth living."

*I*t was not as though Socrates himself had the answers to the questions he raises. Solutions do not emerge from the discussions. But what does emerge is the inability of people who profess to have knowledge to answer the question, "What kind of behavior is good for the soul?" Socrates will admit that he at least is ignorant. That is why the oracle declared him wisest of all. Somehow, presumably during the twenty-four-hour "rapt," he had received a command from God (not necessarily the God of Delphi) to urge everyone who would listen to him, young and old, not to care for their bodies or for their money so much as for their souls and how to make their souls as good as possible.

For centuries the "soul" had been given different names and different interpretations. The various cultures of different civilizations gave widely varying accounts of the soul and would continue to do so for centuries after the time of Socrates. Prior to Socrates the soul had never been considered as something which has knowledge or ignorance, or as the seat of goodness or badness. What makes Socrates' conception of the soul unique among the various doctrines of the time was his associating it with man's normal conscious state. In other words, it was not something that operated when the body slept, or had out-of-body experiences, or was guided by revelation. This concept of the soul was the great discovery which Socrates made, and which earned him fame as the founder of the spiritual view of both knowledge and conduct—in other words, ethics, which for Socrates was a field of exact knowledge and subject to the scientific method.

The modern meanings of "soul" are a far cry from the meanings Socrates attached to the word he used for it—"psyche." Socrates' conception of it lacked the strong moral and religious overtones it acquired through centuries of Christian use. It is true that "psyche" did not lack religious association before he took it over, but he was the first to suggest that it was essentially philosophical and intellectual, rather than religious.

For Socrates the injunction "know thyself"

required knowledge of what the self—the soul—is. Knowing oneself means caring for oneself, determining for oneself what is wise or foolish, what is good or evil. The soul becomes the seat of both goodness and knowledge. Belief is not the same thing as knowledge. It cannot be trusted to guide a person in all circumstances. True knowledge can only be secured by reason. What Socrates found particularly irksome was the pretense to knowledge when grounds for it had not been established.

Now the only thing worth doing is for the sake of the good, and those who know themselves know what things are really good for them—as opposed, for instance, to those things that are only apparently so. The activity of the soul, in other words, provided a direct insight into the value of things we desire. It is not a matter of having true knowledge as opposed to false knowledge. For Socrates true knowledge would be self-evident. False knowledge would be a self-contradiction.

Such a position led Socrates to the belief in the unity of the virtues. Virtue is simply knowledge. And one cannot sin against knowledge. The effect of this is to deny sin a positive quality. It is simply the absence of knowledge, just as darkness is the absence of light. Since one's activities are always directed toward some perceived good, any contrary effect must be the fault of the understanding; it is impossible on this view to make bad use of the knowledge of the good. To do wrong is to damage the soul. Thus it is worse to do wrong than to be wronged, and one should never repay a wrong with a wrong.

This marvelously simple analysis of the soul and its function led to a similarly simple framework for Socrates' ethics. Since virtue was equated with knowledge and vice with ignorance, and since one can not sin against knowledge, all wrong-doing, all error is involuntary. This position, suspiciously deterministic, was to be strongly attacked by Aristotle and others who objected that it freed men of responsibility for their actions. Aristotle would later say of it: "It is irrational to suppose that a man who acts unjustly does not wish to be unjust or a man who acts dissolutely to be dissolute. Wickedness is voluntary, or else we shall have to quarrel with what we have just said and deny that a man is the author and begetter of his actions."

But in fifth century Athens, the idea of self-knowledge had not caught on. Tradition and authority still ruled. But was it the best guide? As for the elders teaching morality, the fact that Pericles' sons amounted to nothing, as well as those of many other great men (and, as it would turn out, the sons of Socrates himself), made it clear to Socrates that education of the young cannot be trusted to authority and custom. Democracy had not improved the condition of people, nor had the imposing accomplishments of the intellect. Society could improve itself, Socrates believed, only if citizens would perform the tasks in society for which their knowledge, talents, training and character best suited them. So far as rulers of states are concerned, Socrates believed that states should no more be run by those who have not mastered that craft anymore than the seas should be crossed by inexperienced mariners.

Socrates was not alone in challenging the authority of the state and the competency of its elders in providing an adequate education for the youth of the city. Fifth century Athens was filled with a new breed of men with strange ideas about the universe.

They had come from Asia Minor and from Southern Italy for decades. They were called Sophists from their concern with wisdom, but many of them were not, strictly speaking, philosophers. The Sophists did not establish a school, nor did they teach a common set of opinions. But they did establish a new profession, that of teaching. Protagoras, the greatest of the Sophists and a friend of Pericles, preached that man is the measure of all things, implying that there are no absolute truths. Socrates believed that man is the measure of all things in the sense that if man were not the measure, if something external to man was, one could never be sure if he were being deceived or not. He disliked the extreme relativism of the Sophists. What Socrates could find appealing in Protagoras was the view that all human conduct—whether applied to making laws, running the state, or governing one's own personal affairs—should be based on intelligent reflection, and not simply on tradition or authority.

There were substantial differences between the Sophists' approach to teaching and that used by Socrates. The most prominent of the Sophists—men like Prodicus and Protagoras—believed like Socrates that the essence of man is reason. But whereas some

Sophists, who were no more than itinerant teachers, often made of reason a game, leading to skepticism or agnosticism, Socrates makes it a search for man's spiritual center. And whereas they taught ethics from a pragmatic, a utilitarian point of view, Socrates taught it as knowledge required for realization of the good: self-interest was identified with material well-being. And whereas the Sophists attempted to teach new rules of conduct, Socrates simply wanted men to acquire a firm understanding of the rules they had already accepted, and to determine whether those rules squared with the duties they could rationally assign themselves. And whereas Sophists sold their knowledge for handsome fees, Socrates would take no money. And whereas they lectured, Socrates' conversants were considered friends or associates entangled in a conversation that involved carefully put questions. For Socrates that was the meaning of philosophy, and it has never known a purer meaning—before or since his time.

The Sophist movement was a popular one in fifth century Athens because of the need for the expansion of learning and the need to apply that learning. For example, because Athenians in Socrates' time were turning more and more to the courts to settle their disputes, training in the art of speaking became highly valued, and the Sophists were masters in the art of rhetoric. Prodicus was said to have a one-*drachma* lecture and a fifty-*drachma* lecture. Socrates once remarked that could he have but heard Prodicus's fifty-*drachma* lecture, he could have learned the truth about the correctness of words.

About words, Socrates actually knew a great deal. In his search for definitions he looked for those to which universal meanings could be attached. Otherwise, particulars could not be designated as belonging to a given class of objects. To be led from the particular to the general was a form of induction by which Socrates tested and rejected hypotheses. But to what extent it served as the basis for Plato's celebrated theory of Forms is much debated. Socrates did not, however, read into general terms any cosmic or metaphysical significance, as Plato was to do. What is clear is that Socrates applied definitions to moral ends. The Sophist practice of using terms that described such ethical ideas as justice, courage, temperance, and the like, and then maintaining that nothing in reality corresponded to those terms was especially troublesome to Socrates. He needed definitions which would make things stay put, especially when considering opinions regarding the nature of virtue, or the moral good. Real virtue, he thought, must have a unifying principle. But he failed to recognize that the common consent of mankind gives only universal opinions, and that validity is attached to definitions only when they are based on the bedrock of Reality.

*T*he Sophist impact on education was significant and generally positive. European humanistic studies have their beginning here. The influence was facilitated by the rapid change in Athens from a poetic to a prose expression, from the spoken to the written word, a process Socrates did not himself engage in, but without which the meaning of his philosophy could not be explicated. When Socrates was a boy, all Athenians were raised on Homer. And, even a century later, Aristotle was educating the young Alexander about Homeric heroes.

But more importantly involved in the new movement was the larger issue of pedagogy. Who was responsible for educating the young? As has been noted, after a brief exposure to "elementary subjects," Athenians were educated by their parents and the adults of the city, not by professionals with subject matter contained in a curriculum. To refer to the "school" of Anaxagoras or the "school" of Archelaus is simply to identify a group of disciples or followers. Plato was the first to establish a school in a higher-education sense. The problem with education had become much more than a matter of handling abstract language; it also had a practical side. But part of that practical side was viewed as negative. In spite of marvelous achievements of the intellect, in spite of the positive promises of democracy, in spite of the force of custom and authority, the new education available in Athens had not made men better. It had, at least in Socrates' mind, made them worse. However one viewed it, it had made Athens a city of talkers.

The solution was a different approach to education. In the minds of many Athenians, the decline and fall of Athens was directly attributable to the removal of tradition and authority as the mainstay of a culture. So Socrates, while different in many ways from the ordinary Sophist, did, in this sense, participate in "corrupting the young." Even worse, at the time of the trial, he would be charged with educating the traitors Critias and Alcibiades—and all this from simply engaging people in conversation and asking some pointed questions.

It is true that the Sophists concerned themselves with the proper conduct of human affairs, but they delighted often, when weighing two sides of a question, of making the weaker side appear the stronger, a practice foreign to Socrates, and disliked by him because it could lead to agnosticism or skepticism. The utilitarian emphasis of Sophism made success the criterion of man's meaning. What is successful justifies any action to achieve it. Time-honored absolutes like truth and justice are replaced by expediency.

Socrates' utilitarianism took the form of believing that the good is only what is useful, and things are useful to different people in different ways. Beauty, too, is related to utility. Things are beautiful to the extent they serve a particular function. For Socrates, then, the beautiful and the good are related, because the relation to a thing that makes something good also makes it beautiful. The Sophists taught goodness, but as a specialized practical exercise. Socrates was not so certain that goodness could be taught. It certainly could not be taught, he thought, by the lecture method used by the Sophists (which would be not unlike a parent lecturing a child). Now if goodness is knowledge and nothing but knowledge, then it can be taught, yet it is not clear how Socrates resolved the problem. But it did involve two people involved in a mutual search for answers, whereby one person helps the other to self-knowledge. Now this seems to involve recovering knowledge that somehow was in the person all along.

To what extent Socrates believed in the immortality of the soul is a much debated question. If the words he uses in Plato's *Apology* are historical, he could be classified as an agnostic. Whether he believed that knowledge is a recollection of a former state or a recognition of a former condition or not, he did believe that the function of the soul is knowledge. Truth resides in the individual. A Socratic questioner simply awakens in people the knowledge that is already there. An assumption is made that the person being questioned has within him the ability to answer questions if they are phrased the right way. But there is also an assumption that if someone has true knowledge of something, he will be able to define it.

To seek to base conduct on knowledge seems an innocent enough pastime, but many Athenians were annoyed by Socrates' persistent questioning of the grounds of their beliefs. Placing the seat of truth in the individual mind was a direct attack on the authority of the state to set the standards for public morality.

Concerning the charge of his being a public nuisance, Socrates had a simple explanation: he was simply following his mother's profession of midwife. (He called it his obstetric art.) "My task," he said, "is to be the midwife to men's souls, not to bear them; that is the work of the God." As midwife, Socrates "brings into the world free men." But his appeal to an "unknown god" sounded strange to Athenian ears. By claiming divine inspirations in matters of conduct, he was seen as challenging the city's authority over religious matters. But to become a midwife Socrates first had to become a gadfly. His own version of that "calling," as repeated by Plato, is a famous one: "[I] am a sort of gadfly, given to the state by God; and the state is a great and noble steed who is tardy in his motions owing to his very size, and requires to be stirred into life. I am that gadfly which God has attached to the State, and all day long and in all places am always fastening upon you, arousing and persuading and reproaching you." That, however, was not an activity for which the Athenians had developed a fondness. Reminding people of their mental and moral deficiency was certain to arouse the indignation of those Athenians superficial enough not to understand Socrates, or those clever enough to have their deficiencies exposed by him.

It is not as though philosophy was natural to Athenians. It had been imported into Athens for almost two hundred years—mainly from the Ionian Coast. So far from being native to Athens was philosophy, in fact, that Socrates and Plato are the only two Athenian philosophers who receive much attention (Aristotle was born in Macedonia and was never accorded the status of citizen).

Socrates' notoriety as a philosopher attracted a wide circle of admirers. Still, he became the subject of burlesque in the plays of the comic playwrights for almost twenty years.

The comic playwright Aristophanes lampooned Socrates with great relish in 423. The date is significant because it marks the first direct reference to Socrates by name before his death. In his play *The Clouds*, Aristophanes represents Socrates as the head of a school of very hard thinkers whose heads are in the clouds (thus the title), a visible form of air in Ionian science, and as such is represented in the chorus. Socrates is also represented as having strange notions about the soul.

In that same year, 423, the comic playwright Ameipsias featured Socrates in a play titled *Connus*, making fun of him—his looks, his dress, his poverty and his ideas—much as Aristophanes had done. Moreover, Socrates was the recurring target of burlesque for the next twenty years, in play after play, attesting to the fact that he was a well-known and controversial figure in Athens.

It is doubtful that any of those "playful" renditions of him reflected the real opinions of any of the attackers. It has even been suggested that Socrates and Aristophanes were on friendly terms, and Ameipsias invited him to appear on the stage; but, in any event, burlesque in classical Attic comedy was always a personal target, not an allusion to a social type as it would later become. The real object of ridicule in *The Clouds* is Ionian science, of which Socrates is represented as its chief spokesman.

So removed were such concepts from the religious beliefs of the average Athenian citizen that it was quite natural for Socrates to become the target of at least five comic poets over an extended period of time. It was not they, however, who brought about his trial and death. It was the degradation of Greek democracy as the result of the conquest of Athens by Sparta, and the disastrous events which attended it.

When Socrates was brought to trial before the King Archon's court, it was because he was perceived to be a danger to a city which was on the verge of collapse. Under such conditions, it was difficult for the threatened community to adhere to its liberal tendencies. Men like Socrates were considered something much more serious than a gadfly. Because of an amnesty protecting the accused against all charges except treason, nothing in Socrates' political past could be used against him. Only twice had he been selected for political service, and both times his actions were offensive to the State. In 406, as a member of a committee of the Senate of the Four Hundred, of which his tribe was a presiding one, he was ordered to try the generals who were charged with dereliction of duty at Arginusae, where twenty-five ships and four thousand men were lost. It was suggested that they be tried as a group, rather than individually, a departure from constitutional procedure. When members of the committee showed reluctance to go along, it was then suggested that their names be included on the list contained in the indictment. Socrates alone refused. The generals were tried and six of them were executed.

In 404 he was ordered, along with four others, to arrest Leon of Salamis, whose property the tyrants intended to confiscate. Again Socrates refused. The others carried out the order. He simply went home, an act punishable by death. He was not, as he was to tell his jurors, cut out for politics. It was clear to the Thirty Tyrants that they had to do something about Socrates, and so they brought charges against him. But the rewriting of the Attic law and the implication of that for the law-courts resulted in a four-year delay. He could not be brought to trial until 400, under charges that, while not totally manufactured, were seriously distorted.

When the charges were filed against Socrates—that he did not believe in the gods of the city, that he introduced new gods, and that he corrupted the youth of the city—they lacked much of the punch they would have carried had not the amnesty not been in effect. The latter charge appears, in spite of Plato's reference to it in the Apology, to be quite unhistorical. The only crimes over which the King Archon's Court had jurisdiction were murder and impiety. Even if the questioning conducted by Socrates had been illegal, it could not have been considered a capital offense by the King Archon's court. But it was well known that Socrates had been the teacher of Critias, the leader of the Thirty Tyrants, and of the traitor Alcibiades, who had defected to Sparta. Because of the amnesty, none of this could be brought out at the trial nor could his dereliction of duty while in politics.

It was customary for those charged with crimes which might result in the death sentence to go into voluntary exile. Those who brought the charges against Socrates were surprised when he did not do so. If a sentence of death were imposed, the accused, by law, could offer an alternative, such as a heavy fine. Socrates suggested as an alternative that he be kept at state expense, and pay a fine of one *mina*. His perceived obstinacy and insolence angered his jurors; but, even so, forty-five percent of them voted for his acquittal. During the thirty-day wait for his execution, he could have escaped, as his friends urged him to do, but he would not. He believed that if men showed contempt for the laws of the city, the city could not survive—a concept of the laws that viewed them as more than mere political expressions. His speeches on this subject, as well as on the occasion of his trial and his death, are among the most moving passages in the literature of Western civilization.

It is not that Socrates placed so little value on his life that he would make no serious effort to save it. He did, after all, have a wife and three children, as well as innumerable friends. But he would not save his life at the expense of his honor and the welfare of the state. The finest expression of his position is contained in the lines from Plato's *Apology*, the record of his trial.

The account of Socrates' last days and death is given by Plato in the *Crito* and the *Phaedo*. The latter concerns the nature of the human soul and its function of acquiring knowledge. It contains some surprising touches of humor, but its most attractive quality is its eloquent expressions regarding man's moral condition. Most scholars agree that "for the portrayal of the end of a good, wise, and just man, who dies without fear, thoughtful of others, and sensitive to the sorrow of his friends, the beauty and poignancy of the *Phaedo* are probably unmatched in the history of literature."

It is not too much to claim, as professor Richmond does, that Socrates combined in his person the spiritual, rational, and moral qualities—representing all that the Greek mind would develop in the ensuing years, though separately, and that "ultimately, all problems of religion and philosophy (whether East or West) all issues concerning the individual and society, Church and State, may be said to meet in him."

Can that be said of any other person?

PLATO

BY
JERRY
ANDERSON

# *Plato*

## 427-347 BC

> "*The true lover of knowledge is always striving after being....He will not rest at those multitudinous phenomena whose existence is appearance only.*"

Plato has exerted more influence on human thought during the entire course of Western civilization than any other historical person, including Aristotle. Even during the centuries when Aristotle's star was in the ascendancy, Plato's thought was conspicuously present; and Aristotle himself claimed to be a Platonist, even though he rejected many of his master's ideas. We are all Platonists, it has been said, whether we like it or not. And that is so because Plato filled the universe with concepts that we have been unable to rid ourselves of.

Plato not only laid the foundation of Western culture, but his influence still retains much of its force. The influence of Christian Platonism has pervaded most of the cultures of Europe, and in one form or another still survives. Jewish and Muslim scholars gave great attention to the writings of Plato as early as the first century after Christ; and although his ideas did not permeate Jewish and Islamic theology to any great extent, they have received respectful consideration for over two thousand years. For the first thousand years his ideas went virtually unquestioned, as those ideas helped to shape the ethics of Christianity. His influence which was notably high in the Middle Ages, increased in the Renaissance, flourished during the ages of Descartes, Berkeley, and Hegel, and is still manifested in the writings of notable thinkers in Europe and America. So pervasive has been his influence, in fact, that all philosophy in the last twenty-three hundred years has been described as a footnote to Plato.

Little is known about the facts of Plato's life, and much of what is known about him only serves to reveal his distaste for democracy as a form of government. By 399 BC Athenian democracy had degenerated to such an extent that it lacked the intellectual and moral discernment necessary to give it credence. With Socrates' death, Plato and other friends and associates of Socrates found it advisable, for reasons of health, to leave Athens until the anti-Socratic feelings could subside.

A principal reason that so little is known of Plato's life—his name is seldom mentioned by his contemporaries, even by Aristotle, who studied in his Academy for twenty years—is that it was considered disrespectful to refer to persons by name in print while they lived, thus delaying the advent of biography. Where his travels took him is not precisely known. He seems to have first gone to Megara where Euclides had a school, and he apparently lived with Euclides for about eight years. There is evidence that he visited Egypt and Cyrene, home of the great mathematician Theodorus, before travelling to the Greek cities of southern Italy and Sicily. In Syracuse, the wealthiest of the Greek cities, he was the guest of Dionysius I.

It is generally thought that he established his famous school, the Academy, in 387, but there are good reasons for believing that it was not established until about ten years after Plato's return to Athens. It is recorded that he lived at the Academy, located about a mile west of Athens, upon his return to his native city; but "Academy" was the name of Plato's house, and he might have taught students there before he established his school, just as he had studied with Euclides in his home at Megara.

Many scholars believe that the Academy was Europe's first university, chiefly on the basis of its broad curriculum. Most of the students came from Greek cities in the Mediterranean area; few were from Athens. Although several subjects of a scientific nature were taught, politics assumed a decidedly important role in the school; and so successful was Plato in training the leaders of cities whose policies were often very heavy-handed, that he was accused of running a school for tyrants. Plato undoubtedly saw himself as fulfilling Pericles' dream of a "School of Hellas." What can unquestionably be claimed for the school is that it was, besides a training school for philosophers, a university with a widely based curriculum, featuring astronomy, biology, science, math, and political science. Moreover, it functioned as a research center, offering a rich program of continuing education.

For some twenty years Plato carried out the program of the school, which included material

presented in his Dialogues. On two occasions, in 367 and 361, he returned to Syracuse, hoping to influence the form of government carried out by Dionysius II. Both attempts were failures, and he was forced to accept the conclusion that his ideal for philosopher-kings could not be implemented in his lifetime, or perhaps, in a thousand lifetimes.

It is impossible to approach Plato except through his writings, all of which, so far as anybody knows, have survived. The reason given for their survival when so many of the ancient texts have been lost is the veneration they inspired, from his time to ours.

Shortly after the birth of Christ, Plato's works were published in their entirety for the first time. Nine collections of four works were assembled for publication. Thirty-five of these are the so-called Dialogues, and the last is a collection of thirteen letters Plato was supposed to have written. The use of the dialogue in literary expression constitutes almost the entire body of his work. No one knows exactly how many dialogues he wrote. Of the thirty-five often attributed to him, six are believed to be spurious and five are in doubt. The *Apology*, a record of the trial of Socrates at which Plato confessed to be present, is only superficially in dialogue form as are large parts of still others.

As a literary device, the dialogue served Plato's interests in advancing the cause of new ideas admirably; but it was not without its problems. Plato actually forbade its use in the Academy for

the first couple of decades of its existence. The reason for such a prescription was the same that got Socrates into trouble with the authorities for his effective use of it: in the hands of a skillful practitioner, the dialogue could have a devastating effect on young minds not yet capable of making careful distinctions; the result often was agnosticism or atheism.

Yet it was probably from necessity that Plato turned to the dialogue as a form of expression. He viewed it as reason revealed by the word. And his own experience with reason dictated that it be expressed through the dialectic, a form that accommodated the tensions of opposing points of view, none of which, apparently, was foreign to the mind of Plato as he struggled to give expression to that great canopy of thought which was so characteristic of the Greek experience.

The so-called Socratic Dialogues include those that deal primarily with the life and thought of Socrates. The *Euthyphro* (before the trial), the *Apology* (the trial), the *Crito* (just prior to Socrates' death), and the *Phaedo* (the death of Socrates) are the best known of these. Over the years Socrates assumed a diminishing role in what are called the early Platonic dialogues, primarily because Plato had discovered his own philosophy, which took him far beyond anything his master had envisioned. The dialogues of the middle Platonic period continued this process as did the later dialogues. By the time he wrote the *Laws*, Socrates had disappeared completely from the dialogues; yet Plato always credited Socrates with inspiration for his work.

**B**y far the most famous work in dialogue form is Plato's *Republic*, a work consisting of several "books." Some scholars claim that it is the most important book ever written by a single author, a strong claim indeed. By any method of reckoning, it is one of the most influential books ever written. His doctrine, based on Socrates' identification of virtue as knowledge, contains elements of religion, of science, of politics, and of legislation; but its unfailing premise is that reason must be followed wherever it leads. The *Republic*, the *Phaedo*, and the *Symposium* are considered Plato's greatest dialogues.

Plato has, over the centuries, received as much praise for the excellence of his prose as for the originality of his ideas. He is considered not only the greatest writer of the Greek language, but one of the greatest in any language. He had tried his hand at painting, at music, at writing verses, and, it is claimed, at composing an epic and a tragedy.

Much has been made of the dramatic quality of the dialogues of Plato, putting him above all of his

contemporaries in the use of this popular form of expression. His skillful delineation of character, his rich vocabulary, his use of rhetoric, his colloquialisms, his uses of humor, irony, pathos, and gravity all reveal him to be a consummate master of his art. The subject matter of his dialogues is given additional life by his skillful use of metaphor, simile, myth, and allegory.

Some of Plato's compositions are written in descriptive style, but his most interesting work is associated with his philosophical thought, which is contained in the conversational form of the dialogue and which involves the combatants in a duel of words—words so effectively used that the reader is often made a participant in the contest by the power of the various moods expressed as well as by the logical merits of the argument.

*T*his wonderful war of words is not waged in the late dialogues, where Plato's prose becomes often dull and lame. Still, Plato's ability to present abstract issues clearly and forcefully is plainly evident as he directs his ideas to a different audience, the students at the Academy.

It is safe to assume that because the oral tradition was still strong in Greek culture that many of Plato's brilliant expressions did not find their way onto the printed page. What he did write was from an obvious love of writing, and its effect was to make him almost the first man of letters. Much of his success as a philosopher and as a writer can be attributed to his remarkable power of intuition which allowed him to escape the limitation of his senses.

But in mixing philosophy and poetry, science and art, Plato runs the risk of being misunderstood. In what character does he reveal himself? Is he in earnest or simply being playful? Almost any attempt to understand Plato runs into serious difficulties, owing to the complexity of his thought, the shifting nature of his philosophy, and the mystical nature of his imagery. He didn't see himself as building a system but he did so all the same. Plato more or less wrestled himself into a system that he himself would not have recognized as such.

Many of Plato's dialogues try to identify the essence of some idea considered to be philosophically important by offering a definition of it. His ethical theory was based on the premise that the good which all people seek is happiness, and that happiness is the realization of something that is natural to man. Just as health can be said to be the natural condition of the body, he argues, virtue is the natural condition of the soul, and happiness can be achieved by virtue or knowledge. "Virtue" did not have the meaning for the

ancient Greek that we assign to it, but, for that matter, neither did "soul." Virtue was considered to be that which constituted the excellence of a person, that which expressed the rightness of a life. It was the sum of all virtues, the chief of which were wisdom, justice, courage, and temperance. Virtue, though, is best expressed as a single thing rather than as different things. And it is teachable only to the extent that it is identified with knowledge. The soul, on the other hand, was the seat of virtue. Plato often used it in the sense of "mind."

In his depiction of the soul, Plato's chief aim was to demonstrate that sense experience could not serve as the basis for either knowledge or reality. Reason alone could lead the individual to an understanding of the universal principles which existed in a hierarchical order. The truly good is the rational analysis of values. Pleasure cannot be counted on to produce virtue and happiness, just as sense expressions cannot yield truth. Indulging our desires is not the same as satisfying our needs. Itching and scratching can hardly be described as a principle for guiding conduct. A soul was needed for that.

Plato constructs the soul on the threefold classification he used for his Ideal State. Just as the State depends on the harmonious interplay of three distinct classes, each with its own function to perform, so the soul is described as having an appetitive element (the cravings of sense), a rational element (which is possessed solely by man), and, between these higher and lower elements, an element which is capable of controlling the lower element and taking orders from the higher. It is this "spiritedness" which drives us to action. That we are creatures of desire Plato never denied, but the appetites and man's spiritedness must be controlled by reason, which, as the highest and noblest part of our nature, can be trusted to give direction to our life.

As important as this description of the soul was in establishing a metaphysical principle for Plato's ethics, it took on even greater significance in the later dialogues as Plato attempted to find a suitable realm for the soul. Before he could do this, he needed to work out his vision of the eternal Ideas which would explain all the disparate elements present in the universe.

How Plato arrived at his notion of "eternal Ideas" is a matter of great importance, and it helps to explain the progressive nature of his thought. He took from Socrates the idea that particulars do not provide the essence of reality. To escape the relativistic notions of particular opinions, Socrates has sought to combine them under universal definitions which could be known for certain and allow the mind to escape the limitations of sense perception. Many scholars believe, however, that while such ideas became the genesis of Plato's treatment of Ideas and Forms, they carried no such metaphysical significance for Socrates, who was content to remain an earthbound moralist and to seek out teleological rather than mechanical explanations of the world.

In addition to the influence of Socrates, other widely-held notions had influenced Plato's thinking. He had from the time he was a boy been caught up in the opinion of the Heraclitean school that all objects of sense are in perpetual flux, and thus no real knowledge of them is possible. This was a position which Plato never really abandoned, but he did supplement it with additional ideas—such as those provided by the Pythagorean philosophy which was based on mathematics, and whose origins were mystical and religious. Plato had also accepted the doctrine of Parmenides that reality is timeless and eternal, and that, as a result, all change is illusory. Combining this concept with Heraclitus' notion that there is nothing which escapes change in the world of the sense, Plato was led to conclude that knowledge can be gained only by the intellect, which recognizes the permanency of the Forms or Ideas. All of this fit in well with his wholesale adoption of Pythagoras' ideas about immortality, other-worldliness, and religious mysticism.

It is almost universally allowed that the "eternal Ideas" were Plato's brilliant, original discovery. Probably no single philosophical concept has so captured the imagination of the entire world. A better word, however, is "Forms," because "Ideas" suggest something mental, something depending on consciousness for its existence. For Plato the "Idea" was no more a product of the mind than it was a product of the material world. If all sensible objects ceased to exist and if all minds or intellects ceased to exist, for Plato the Idea would remain.

Still, the terms "Forms" and "Ideas" are often used as synonyms by scholars when dealing with the subject. Plato himself describes the Forms as eternal and immutable, present in all time and in all places, self-identical, self-existent, absolute, separate, simply without beginning and without end. They are complete, perfect, fully existent. They are removed from sense or image, invisible, comprehended only by the mind. With such a description, Plato had elevated the status of Forms assigned to them by Socrates to the level of metaphysical principles, where they would serve as the unshakable foundation for his political and ethical theories. But by doing so, Plato assigned them a role that went far beyond the scope of ethics to which Socrates was content to restrict them. In Plato's hands, they became the intelligible structure of the entire universe. He now had given expression to the view of his former teacher Euclides that the character and existence of a thing was its universal, not its particular essence.

From the perspective of "intelligible structure," Forms become valuable as instruments of classification. A Form is present whenever two or three objects of sense are collected under a common name. For example, Tom, Dick, and Harry collectively yield the Form of Man. Because the number of classes formed by the individuals which comprise them is limitless, the number of Forms is limitless.

Plato mentions Forms not only of natural objects like beds and tables, but of physical qualities like health, and color, and sound, and swiftness. And he mentions Forms of ethical values like justice, and esthetic values like beauty. He also discovers Forms of categories and relations, like sameness and difference. Now taken together, these Forms, when properly arranged by the intellect, constitute a single, coherent system of Reality.

Where Plato did not abandon Socrates' view of Forms was in the conception of them as ideals. Man as an Idea was thus more than a generalized portrait of all the Toms, Dicks, and Harrys—he was an idealized picture relieved of all his imperfections. As ideals, the Forms were objects of adoration. They had a divinity attached to them which attracted the human soul and gave it a solace that sensible objects could not give. Judged from this perspective, the Form of Forms, or Form of the Whole, can readily be viewed in the way God is viewed in theistic religion, although that is only one meaning Plato was to attach to God.

In arranging his Ideas or Forms to other Ideas or Forms in the intelligible world, Plato produces a hierarchy of Forms which reaches from the inanimate world of sense to the highest Ideas from which truth and knowledge are derived. This Plato calls the Idea of the Good. All Ideas have their source in the Good. Good is not identical with truth nor with knowledge. It transcends them both. It is what gives the other ideas their being, their character. Thus, metaphysics, ethics, and esthetics all point to the Good. At this point it becomes evident that Plato's twofold universe of things and Forms has become a threefold universe of things, the Forms, and the Good.

It must be remembered that such notions were not just the subject matter of his dialogues— notably the *Phaedo*, the *Republic*, and the *Phaedrus*. He taught such ideas in his school, and he encountered substantial opposition to them. Never so great a mystic that he could not sense the problems that his views engendered, he could not shake the nagging suspicion that the Forms could not exist without real involvement in the world of sense. Nor was it enough to suggest that objects of sense were "shadows" or poor copies of Forms, as Aristotle was quick to point out. To say that Form "participated" in objects or "resembled" them did not clear up the problem of the relations of Form to concrete objects. And the relation of Form to mind posed problems of still a different kind.

Ideas or Forms were particularly important for Plato because they were the means for seeing things as they really are, and, therefore, the basis for knowledge. To give a clearer idea of the reality that underlies physical things, consider a coin that a person finds while walking on the beach. If the face value of the coin were printed in a language that the finder did not understand, he would still have an idea of it as a coin because of its form. But if the finder of the coin did not know what money is, he would not see it as a coin simply because he would lack the idea of it. The reality of the thing, then, is not in what one perceives as a particular object, but in what those objects transmit as Ideas or Forms. In other words, Plato is suggesting that we cannot know individual things as anything except as an expression of a more general thing which reveals itself to us as an Idea or Form. But Ideas and Forms are not things; they do not reside in the world. They are not directly accessible to our conscious minds. Still, they are within us in some way. So how do we know them? The answer is given in one of Plato's most widely known and highly regarded myths.

In the *Phaedrus*, Socrates tells how the soul in the original condition was comparable to a chariot pulled by two winged horses, one a thoroughbred who reacted to the reins as it was instructed to do (our tractability); the other horse was wild and ungovernable (our passions and sexual instincts), always trying to escape from its traces. The driver of the chariot, who is represented by reason, struggles to keep the two horses pulling together as the chariot travels through the realm of Ideas, which the soul contemplates and understands. But owing to the actions of the unruly horse, the chariot falls, the horses lose their wings, and the soul becomes incarnated in the physical body.

Now depending on how well the souls before their fall caught the vision of the Ideas, they are assigned to bodies in a hierarchal order of nine positions, with the philosopher occupying the highest position and the tyrant occupying the lowest.

It is clear from this that Plato gives an account of the origin of man as a result of the fall of the soul from a sphere (heaven) where the soul has lost its memory of the Ideas. When the soul catches imaginatively only a glimpse of the Ideas, memory is stimulated, and the aching stumps of his wings are agitated, causing him to wish to return to his celestial home. Still, things remain but shadows of Ideas, sufficiently to remind us of the perfect Forms by which they remain poor representations. Plato has made of man a fallen being, but a being who, having seen the Ideas, has a certain affinity with them.

In addition to his description of the soul as a two-part entity, having a higher and a lower nature, other important ideas emerge from Plato's myth. The first is that the soul is immortal; the second is that knowledge is reminiscence. Knowledge is internal because it is a process of remembering. But to know truth, the soul must have some sort of affinity with it, and that affinity is ancestral. In both the *Phaedo* and the *Phaedrus*, Plato had made the soul the seat of the process of knowledge, and had described it as both uncreated and immortal. It was not, however, until the later dialogues that Plato made of the soul a cosmic principle, assigning it as an intermediary between the Forms and the sensible world. As such the soul made possible the relation of Forms to the objects of the physical world.

*P*lato's second great myth is the "Myth of the Cave." It involves prisoners in an underground cave (the world of the senses), doomed to watch the flickering shadows (data of the senses), which are cast by figures behind them. These figures are physical objects on the surface of the earth (the intelligible world) which in turn are copies of the Ideas which exist in the sunlight above. What the prisoners see is nothing but a shadow of an image. But this is what they take for truth. Now if the prisoners are turned to face the firelight, they will have difficulty making out the figures. They will have even more difficulty believing that the figures are more real than the shadows. When taken up into the sunlight, they will be even more dazzled and blinded. Eventually, they distinguish the objects (the Ideas, or Forms), of which the figures are merely copies. And, after a long time of fixing their gaze on the Ideas which constitute reality, their philosophically trained eye can bear to look upon the Idea of the Good (which is analogous to the sun in the sensible world).

Plato doesn't really believe that truth can be discovered by the mind while it is imprisoned in the body. What is required is a "conversion" of the mind from the world of sense to the world of intelligible Ideas. Knowledge of this kind comes only by way of an indescribable ecstasy, a mystical union; but it can have no meaning unless the object of knowledge—the universal and absolute—has real being.

That same process which brings about the consummation of knowledge is required for the consummation of love, and perhaps no doctrine of Plato's philosophy has been given more reverential treatment than his concept known as Platonic love. Professor Julian Marias notes that the Greeks had three principle words for love. The term *eros* was used to refer to the desire for what one does not have and misses. It was, for the most part, a longing for beauty. *Philia* was used to signify friendship and companionship. Aristotle chose it for philosophy—the love of wisdom. *Agape*, the third term for love, had to do with a mutual regard for one another, expressing esteem and warmth. It took on special significance during early Christianity, becoming *caritas* or charity.

So, what is the importance of recalling the different meanings of love that the Greeks attached to the term? It is that Plato, Aristotle, and Augustine all used a different meaning of love as the way to philosophy: for Plato philosophy was reached through *eros*; for Aristotle, through *philia*; and for Augustine, through *caritas (agape)*. *Non intratur in veritatem nisi per caritatem,* says Augustine. "No one can enter truth except through charity."

It would be difficult to say which one of these approaches to love has had the most influence over the centuries, but it is safe to assert that Plato's version is the most mystical if not the most spiritual.

In the *Symposium*, the only dialogue in which a woman plays a significant part, the theme is "love," as it is in the *Phaedrus*, and the dialogue features a tribute to the god Eros. Diotima teaches that love is something halfway between men and the gods. Wisdom is knowledge of the most beautiful things, and love is love of the beautiful. At the top of Plato's hierarchy of Forms, as we have seen, is the Idea of the Good. Just below it is truth, and next comes beauty. Because beauty is more visible then truth, it can lead us to truth. From the contemplation of the beauty of a particular body, we are led to the beauty of bodies in general, then to the beauty of soul, and finally to the beauty of Ideas. When we reach that level, we have knowledge—*sophia*. In the embrace of this absolute beauty, we fulfill our longing for immortality.

It is important to note that Plato does not minimize the importance of the first step in this process—the love of particular, physical bodies. The universals depend on the particulars for their existence, just as the particulars depend on the universals as Ideas or Forms. To put the case another way, "Platonic love" is not a rejection of erotic passion, if by "Platonic love" is meant a purely spiritual relationship which does not admit physical attraction. But Plato does insist that the desire for physical contact be subordinated to the loftier ideal of appreciating the beauty that underlies all human beings and makes for good human relationships. While physical love may perpetuate the species, a more beautiful offspring is generated, suggests Plato, by those who govern cities and shape the moral characteristics of future generations.

These last two expressions of love are the basis of Plato's ideas about politics and ethics. Almost half of his entire work is devoted to politics in some form, and the fullest expression of it appears in the *Republic*, Plato's longest work. Plato did not separate politics and ethics. One was simply an expression of the other on a grander scale. The first book of the *Republic* takes up the question of justice. Here Plato argues against the contention of Thrasymachus that there is no natural right and that morality is merely the interest of the party in power at the moment. Private morality, in Thrasymachus' view, is only a form of selfishness which works against the interest of the state, making it inadvisable for citizens to pursue their private interests. What Plato is eager to combat is the notion that morality is artificial and a matter of expediency. To do so he must establish a positive view of righteousness, or, as he calls it, "justice."

Plato thinks that the ideal State can best be described as the individual "writ large." By raising the search for righteousness to the political level, we can recognize it more easily. He begins by dividing the state into classes—a working class, an army to defend it, and a governing class. The State, he says, should be limited in size and wealth. He would have women receive the same training as men, even military training. He would abolish marriage and private property among the governing class. Within this class, only men between twenty-five and fifty-five should be allowed to father, and only women between twenty and forty should be allowed to bear children. Union would be by lot, but the deck is stacked so that the bravest and best men are paired with the strongest and fairest women. Inferior children would be put out of the way at birth, and the others would be separated from their mothers and brought up by the State. They would be placed in a government nursery and remain ignorant of the identity of their parents. This practice would eliminate the private interest that the family creates.

But the most far-reaching proposal in this description of an ideal State—hereafter known as a Utopia—is that the rulers should be philosophers. Plato describes a rigid outline of training for the would-be rulers that lasts for no less than twenty-five years. Twenty years are spent on preparatory studies of music and gymnastics, fields having a much broader significance than are presently attached to them. At age thirty, the pupil is subjected to five years of dialectic or philosophy. Then follows fifteen years of practical life and of governing the State. At age fifty governors are released from their duties and allowed to return to a contemplative life befitting philosopher-kings.

*I*n his description of the education provided to the governing class, Plato sets forth a remarkable theory of the relationship of art to morality.

Homer and Hesiod, Greece's two greatest poets, were to be banned because of their irreverent treatment of the gods. The pupils should be exposed to nothing that is not morally uplifting and a model of virtue. That means that dramatic poetry too must be carefully censored. Since dramatic poetry is imitative, it must always imitate that which is good. Even the epic poet is required to utter only that which a strict moralist would allow. Music fared no better. Lydian and Ionian melodies are too soft or too often used for drinking songs and must be forbidden. The Dorian and Pyrygian modes, however, are stern and serious enough to be allowed. All arts must have only one aim—moral edification.

By the tenth book of the *Republic*, Plato is ready to fire the fatal volley at art, a conclusion that his moral fundamentalism makes inescapable: all art is bad. It imitates the sensible world which itself imitates the reality of the Ideas. So it is an imitation of an imitation. It is an inferior who marries an inferior and has inferior offspring. Poetry is especially poor stuff, calling up, as it does, unworthy emotions.

Despite the brilliant exposition of the soul contained in the *Phaedo*, the *Phaedrus,* and the *Republic*, and of the ideal commonwealth described in the Republic, it is unwise to think that these represented any kind of finality in Plato's thought. He reacted constantly to public opinion and to the realities of the political state of affairs.

The *Timaeus*, containing as it does an exposition of cosmology, physics, and biology, was used for years as a science textbook at the Academy. In the *Statesman* and the *Laws*, Plato reveals his ability to adapt to social reality. In the former he argues still that monarchy is the best form of government, but that it should be limited by constitutional restraints. He allows that the kind of constitution adopted by a state is not as important as the kind of statesmanship displayed by the ruler. Aristocracy controlled by law would be the next best form, constitutional democracy the least preferable. Without the control imposed by law on all three forms of government, they would express themselves as tyranny, oligarchy, and mob-rule.

In his last dialogue, the incomplete *Laws*, Plato sets out the rules and regulations to which a state should be subjected. Laws are more important, now, for Plato than is the kind of constitution a state adopts. But since God is recognized as the foundation of the State as well as its head, the rules should be those that God would approve. Plato deals at length with laws pertaining to both the civil and criminal spheres, and he describes in great detail the political and judicial mechanism required for running and maintaining law and order. In civil matters, the rules apply to marriage, the family, the conduct of business, ownership of property. In the criminal field, crimes are described and their punishment prescribed. Education is treated pretty much as it was in the *Republic*, with the arts retaining the same level of disapproval because of their demoralizing effect.

By now Plato's State is theocratic. Its governance has shifted from relaxed to austere. Plato himself has become puritanical, at times fanatical. The playfulness and charm and wit so apparent in the early dialogues are gone. He died at age 80, while still working on the *Laws*.

Despite the difference between the *Laws* and the earlier dialogues, the essential claim of Platonism has always remained the same: the existence of a spiritual and intelligible reality that is independent of the physical world, and is the cause of that world and of the values it embraces.

Upon Plato's death in 347, Aristotle wrote an elegy, praising him as "the man for whom it is not unlawful for even bad men to praise, who alone of mortals clearly revealed, by his own life and by the methods of his words, how to be happy is to be good."

ARISTOTLE

BY
JERRY
ANDERSON

# *Aristotle*
## 384-322 BC

"*All men by nature deserve to know" for each of us is to be identified with his mind and "the activity of the mind is life."*

Since the fourth century before Christ, Aristotle has been one of the most important intellectual figures in Western thought, and one of two greatest intellectual giants produced by the Greeks, the other being Plato. Aristotle's thought was directed by his sense of the reality which existed independently of either opinions or desires, and by his deep trust in the ability of human reason to know this reality as it is. And these convictions account for his readiness to follow empirical facts wherever they might lead. By whatever standard he is judged—originality, breadth or depth of learning, or influence—he stands unique in the whole history of philosophy. In intellectual matters, it is claimed, he formed the European mind.

Throughout his life Aristotle was driven by a single overwhelming desire to learn—to promote the discovery of truth and to increase the sum of human knowledge. He once wrote, "All men by nature desire to know" for each of us is to be identified with his mind and "the activity of mind is life." Speaking chiefly of his own convictions, he stated, "The acquisition of wisdom is pleasant; all men feel at home in philosophy and wish to spend time on it, leaving all other things aside."

In Aristotle's case, the desire for knowledge resulted in a mastery of every field of learning known to the Greeks, including physics, chemistry, biology, zoology and botany; including psychology, political theory, and ethics; including logic and metaphysics; and including history, literary theory, and rhetoric.

His influence has permeated the work of scientists and philosophers throughout the ages. In philosophy his seminal work helped to establish the chief positions of Stoicism, Epicureanism, New-Plationism, Gnosticism, and Scholasticism—in fact all the philosophical systems developed by medieval and modern thinkers, such as Aquinas, Leibnitz, Descartes, Kant, Hegel, Hartmann, and a host of other contributors to the history of Philosophy—in our own century, for example, Frederick Copleston and Mortimer J. Adler.

Plato, in whose Academy Aristotle studied for twenty years, made several references to Aristotle, calling him the intellect of the school, and naming him "the reader" because of his penchant for studying. By the thirteenth century, he was known simply as "the philosopher," reflecting the common acceptance of this most gifted of Plato's disciples as the greatest of all philosophers; and, for Dante, he was "the master of those that know."

It is, therefore, really not an exaggeration to claim that Aristotle, more than any other thinker, determined the direction and form of Western intellectual history. In a real sense, a history of European thought is a history of Aristotle's contributions and influence.

Aristotle is especially valued for his unparalled ability to classify all sciences. His division of knowledge into special branches or "sciences" is still used today, and his "sciences" are now regarded as separate disciplines. But, in Aristotle's time, all knowledge was encompassed by philosophy, the love of wisdom in all its forms—whether of nature, man, or God. Not until the sciences and other disciplines accumulated enough of a body of knowledge to establish themselves as distinct from one another did they break away from philosophy and take on an independent status.

Just as no one before him contributed so much to learning, scarcely any one after him has rivaled his diversity, although the exact record of his output is not known. Ancient catalogs list 170 separate works. In antiquity his works would have required several hundred rolls, containing over one thousand entries that we would call "chapters." Of those 170 works, forty-seven survive, filling about two thousand printed pages.

How they survived is not fully known. The Peripatetic School lost its importance, and the writings of Aristotle were neglected. In the first century BC, the school turned its attention to textual criticism and interpretation, a task begun by Tyrannio and Andronicus of Rhodes, and carried on for many centuries. This movement was responsible for the preservation and transmission of Aristotelian writings. From about 500 AD to 1100, knowledge of his philosophy was almost completely lost in the West. Only the *Logic* survived, and then only in commentaries. But knowledge of his philosophy was preserved by Arab and Syrian scholars who reintroduced it to Western Europe in the 1100's and 1200's.

One of the great Aristotelian scholars of the thirteenth century, Albertus of Cologne, became the teacher of Thomas Aquinas, who based all his work on Aristotle's method. And though subsequent Latin and Arab scholars were responsible for helping to subvert Aristotle's method, it is claimed that something good resulted from their error: they saved the medieval mind from mysticism.

Many of the lost works are known by title and by later references to them. *On Philosophy* (which survives only in fragments) is important because it raised philosophy to the status of a profession. In it Aristotle identifies five principal stages of civilization, with "philosophy" as the final, most perfect stage.

*On Philosophy* is important too, because it represents a pivotal point in Aristotle's life. It was, perhaps, the last of Aristotle's writings which could be classified as strictly "literary"—a work that affirmed the values of the world. Soon after, Aristotle turned to research and teaching and the writing of more technical treatises, such as the *Organon* and the *Physics*.

No one knows the order of Aristotle's writings. They were not written in the order given them by Andronicus of Rhodes, the last head of the Lyceum, who attempted to systemize them in the middle of the first century before Christ; but the order given by Andronicus is still employed today.

The existing writings were never edited by Aristotle; they were, in fact, never intended for publication. He never wrote a work called *Metaphysics*. What he did write was a number of short treatises on the theory of causes and other subjects that were collected into one large treatise and given the name "Metaphysics" to suggest that they should be read after (*meta*) the *Physics*. This method of ordering Aristotle's work accounts in part for the lack of unity, clear progression of thought, repetitions, and even inconsistencies and contradictions.

Aristotle is difficult to read, at times tortuous. Part of this is due to the flexibility of his style, which reflected the flexibility of his thought. In his twelve years at the Lyceum, he often changed his opinion on the subject under investigation. He seemed simply to have added his new line of thinking without bothering to delete the old.

*H*is extant work is a collection of lecture notes—his or his students'. The style is curt, abrupt, and academic, full of unexplained terms and abbreviations intended only for the ears or eyes of those versed in the subject matter. The language is careless and conversational; the exposition is often incomplete, sometimes redundant, sometimes inconsistent. Often what is begun is dropped and what is promised is not delivered. It is remarkable that such a collection of writings—possibly informal records of oral teachings addressed to a few advanced pupils- could have so profoundly influenced the thought of so many centuries. These treatises, called the *esoteric* works (they were sometimes called the *achromatic* writings), were intended only for use by students at the Lyceum

Not all of Aristotle's writings were written in the style of his surviving works. He wrote numerous dialogues modeled after Plato's which were famous for their lucidity and easy flow of style. Cicero was referring to Aristotle's popular treatises (now lost) when in his *Academia* he spoke of the "suave style of Aristotle—a river of gold." One of these treatises was the *Protrepticus*, written while Aristotle was still a student at Plato's Academy. Fashioned after a part of Plato's *Euthydemus*, it became the model for Cicero's *Hortensius*, which Augustine claimed aroused him from his dogmatic slumbers. The ancients, such as the Romans Cicero, Quintilian, and Halicarnassus, knew Aristotle best by these popular treatises, which were called the *exoteric* writings. They were intended for the general public, for those outside the school.

A third group of Arisotle's writings, the *hyponematic*, or memoranda, were used as aids to memory and survive only in fragments. They were largely the collections of research materials and historical records, and were intended as sources of information for scholars. On the basis of these works, Aristotle is credited with being the father of research, although he did not prepare all the material himself. His research included such things as summaries of the teaching of philosophers, a list of victors of the Olympic and Pythian games; a chronology of Athenian dramas–and there were hundreds of them–by date, title, and author; and a collection of 158 constitutions of cities and tribes, most of them Greek (with the recently discovered sole surviving one on the Athenian Constitution probably written by Aristotle himself).

The real unity of Aristotle's work is to be found in his method, his style, and the intellectual character of everything he investigated. His approach to philosophy is open, rather than dogmatic. The weight of his argument is not so compelling as the subtlety of his arguments, his ideas, and his analyses.

Aristotle did not presume that all inquiry would be easily satisfied with a high degree of precision. He takes into account the opinions that ordinary people might hold on his area of investigation. He employs simple words and phrases to identify his key terms. Our language is rich in the words he introduced–"form" and "matter," "substance" and "essence," "quantity" and "quality," "genus" and "species." Aristotle is careful to avoid constructing theories in advance of collecting data. Assembling puzzles and evaluating difficulties, he works his way carefully through the maze of thought with which his subjects were invariably clothed.

In all his treatises, he tried to relate his own views to the whole history of thought which preceded him. Besides solving the problems presented by Plato, he hoped to establish a permanent body of knowledge; yet, as generally acknowledged, his treatises remain an inspiration rather than a final assessment. His method was not based exclusively on deduction, though that became an area of great emphasis during the Middle Ages. For Aristotle, deduction itself was grounded in inductive experiences.

His method was often *aporetic*, that is, based on puzzles or problems to be faced, not necessarily resolved, and it includes the investigation

and classification of "phenomena." Although Aristotle begins with phenomena, for him the word "phenomena" had different uses in different contexts. In biology, meteorology, and astronomy the phenomena under investigation are usually empirical observations made by Aristotle himself or taken from other sources he considered reliable. In ethics, on the other hand, and in his analysis of the basic concepts of physics and psychology, the phenomena being treated are of the same kind as those which underlie the argument of Plato's dialogues: the common convictions or the common linguistic usage of his contemporaries, supplemented by the views of other thinkers.

It is perhaps easiest to explore Aristotle as a philosopher by tracing his activities in the various cities he visited in order to teach and to carry out his researches. Although almost nothing is known of Aristotle's earliest years, it is a matter of record that he was born in 384 BC in Stagira, a town in Macedonia. His father, Nichomachus, was court physician to the grandfather of the man who would become known as Alexander the Great. Because both of his parents died while he was still young, he was brought up by a relative, Proxemus.

In 367, when he was seventeen or eighteen, he was sent to Athens to study in Plato's Academy, which he attended until Plato's death in 348/7. While there he wrote and spoke for Plato's school against the ideas of the school of Isocrates, a politico-rhetorical sophist. Isocrates had insisted upon rhetoric being regarded as a topic which provided a complete education. Aristotle's lectures belittled such an approach, and he was viewed by Isocrates' followers as being simply a mouthpiece for Plato.

While at the Academy, Aristotle showed great interest in the Platonic doctrines which are apparent in Aristotle's works, and in the dialectal

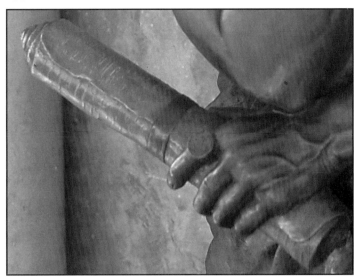

style of writing made popular by Plato—the manner of a dialogue by the exchange of arguments. The dialectic approach is used much more often by Aristotle than the syllogistic approach which he perfected but did not invent.

After Plato's death Aristotle accepted an invitation from Hermeias, a friend of Aristotle at Plato's Academy, to join a new branch of the Academy at Assus in Asia Minor. It is in one of the early chapters of the *Politics*, written at Assus, that Aristotle set forth the view that only the Greeks can live the philosophical life and that non-Greeks are by nature fit to be slaves or serfs. (It is difficult for citizens of enlightened societies to understand how so rational a mind could have arrived at such an irrational conclusion.) Also, at this time,

Aristotle composed the work *On Kingship*, in which he argues that it is best for kings to follow the advice of philosophers, not to attempt to become them. Unlike Plato, Aristotle separated philosophers and kings in the ideal commonwealth.

While at Assus, Aristotle married Phythius, the adopted daughter or niece of Hermias. In the *Politics* Aristotle sets forth the ideal ages for marriage as eighteen for women and thirty-seven for men. Since at this time Aristotle was thirty-seven, it can only be surmised that Phythius was eighteen.

After three years at Assus, Aristotle left for Mytilene on the island of Lesbos, where he spent the next two years carrying out meticulous research in biology. Biology had long been thought to be an inferior subject for study, but Aristotle helped to create an interest in the study of plants and animals. Even at this stage of his career, however, Aristotle did not sacrifice observation to theory, but he had not forgotten his old teacher.

His work in biology led him to theorize upon the relation of the soul to the body. He describes the soul as "the first actuality of a natural body furnished with organs." In his treatise *On the Soul*, Aristotle takes a position opposite to that of Plato, arguing that the soul is the vital, life-giving force of the body, giving the body its form. The body, then, was the material substance of the soul. Together body and soul formed the individ-

ual person. In rejecting the Platonic doctrine that the soul is imprisoned in the body, Aristotle established his own identity in the history of ideas.

After his two-year stay in Mytilene, Aristotle, now forty-two, was invited by King Philip to Pella, the capital of Macedonia, to become tutor to the young Alexander who was then thirteen. Because Aristotle's father had been court physician for Phillip's father, it is possible that Aristotle played with Philip as a child, and that his invitation to tutor Alexander was based on that relationship as much as on his reputation as a scholar. There is no evidence, however, that Alexander put Aristotle's principles into practice. The two had little in common. Aristotle did attempt to model Alexander on the heroes of Homer's *Iliad*, and he prepared an edition of Homer for the young Alexander.

Three years at the fierce, uncivilized Macedonian court were enough for Aristotle, and about 339, when Alexander was appointed regent, he returned to Stagira, his home town, where he continued his association with his friends from Plato's Academy. Though he still considered himself to be a Platonist, Aristotle's thought had developed into a new direction, definitely opposed to that of Plato's successors at the Academy.

Returning to Athens about 335, Aristotle, with some of his friends, particularly Theophratus who was to succeed him as head, opened the Lyceum, a gymnasium attached to the temple of Apollo Lyceus in a grove of olive trees outside Athens, which served as a public garden. The garden itself was already popular with teachers and sophists, and was reported to have been a favorite haunt of Socrates. Aristotle's Lyceum is often referred to as the Peripatetic School, so named because of Aristotle's habit of walking as he lectured. Some scholars insist that the Lyceum, not the Academy, was the world's first university by defining a university as an institution where different subjects are organized and coordinated by a leader who sees to everything. Plato, they argue, did not exercise that kind of leadership.

Aristotle headed up the daily activities of the Lyceum for twelve or thirteen years. The main courses were biology and history, but Aristotle devoted himself to a program of investigation and speculation in almost every branch of inquiry as well as to the composition of most if not all of the scientific writings that are extant.

When Alexander died in Babylon in 323, Aristotle's connection with Macedonia received new interest, and this, possibly, reinforced by opposition in Athens to Aristotle's philosophical opinions, exposed him to the fate of Socrates. He hurriedly left Athens so the Athenians would not, as he put it, "sin twice against philosophy." He fled Athens to settle in Chalcis in Euboea, where his mother had property. He died a year later, in 322, at the age of sixty-two or sixty-three.

The influence of Plato on Aristotle is difficult to assess. That Plato admired Aristotle is clear enough from the many references the teacher makes of his student. But because Aristotle's philosophy often contrasts so sharply with Plato's it has been suggested that Aristotle only gradually modified his views over the course of his career, moving slowly from idealism to empiricism.

The Aristotelian scholar Zürcher suggests that there was no evolution of Aristotle's thought, that Aristotle's thought was always Platonic—Aristotle remained with Plato for twenty years—and that most of Aristotle's extant work was written by Theophrastus, his lifelong friend and colleague.

Zürcher's views are considered too far off course to win many adherents, but they do indicate the difficulty in attaching specific meaning to certain passages encountered in Aristotle's writings. Points of view from different stages of Aristotle's career can be found in a single chapter, even in a single paragraph of his work. This is particularly true with the *Politics* and the *Metaphysics*. Strong anti-Platonic elements that crop up in such early works as the *Topics* and the *Eudaimonian Ethics* compound the difficulty. It is worth noting, too, that simple acceptance of Plato's views was not characteristic of his students nor of Plato himself.

Aristotle's views are, more likely than not, generally evolutionary, particularly in the treatment of subjects like the soul. But he always seemed to maintain an admiration for some of Plato's ideas. He believed, however, that Plato and his pupils were too readily disposed to simplify data, failing to see that a word could hold different meanings when applied to different subjects, or that different topics called for different standards of rigor in arguments. It was certainly not a matter of the empiricist Aristotle opposing the idealistic, spiritualist Plato, although Plato's synoptic ideal of knowledge and Aristotle's idea that branches of science and philosophy should be autonomous seem miles apart.

To reconcile the differences between Plato and Aristotle, it was thought necessary to divide the universe into a world of changeless things and a world of changing things. Bonaventura, for example, thought Plato and Aristotle complemented one another, with Plato treating of eternal things and Aristotle of temporal things, thus bringing about a reconciliation which pre-

pared the way for the Christian philosophy of Saint Augustine. In the nineteenth century, Coleridge, following Bonaventura's principle of distribution, divided everyone into Platonists and Aristotelians, assigning science to Aristotle and innate truths and actual ideas to Plato.

It is one thing to attempt a reconciliation of Plato and Aristotle and quite another to argue, as did Zürcher, that there was never any disagreement between the two. Aristotle, by means of his treatises, was able to construct a system that avoided the inconsistencies and difficulties of Plato's Ideas or Forms. Perhaps the chief difference is that Plato tended to refer everything in nature and human conduct to the supreme idea of Good, and work down through the hierarchy of Forms. Aristotle, on the other hand, tended to refer everything to observable facts, and work upward through the hierarchy of Forms. But the real, and not merely apparent, differences between the two men can be found in a comparison of their work on ethics, politics, and art, as the subsequent treatment of those themes will demonstrate.

The one area of study where Aristotle's originality was fully to express itself was in the life sciences. He invented the science of biology. After 2300 years, he still ranks as one of the greatest biologists of all time. As the founder of systematic and comparative zoology, he surveyed the whole range of the field and provided broad classifications still used today. Zoologists say he was extremely competent in his knowledge of fishes of the Aegean, of which he classified a surprisingly large number. He was acquainted with over five hundred different kinds of animals and had dissected and closely investigated about fifty kinds. He insisted that whales were animals; he understood the principle of biological locomotion, the process of digestion in ruminants, the habits of bees, and the process of animal reproduction. His contributions to mathematics were negligible, not because he had no interest in them, but because he was content to make use of the pronouncements of his contemporaries.

As one might expect, Aristotle lost his reputation as the world's foremost scientist as new means of inquiry and verification were discovered. For Aristotle, nature is dynamic, purposeful, and qualitative. Today's mechanism theory in scientific thought may suggest that Aristotle's views were archaic and naive; but recent theories about subatomic physics have tended to lend credence to his dynamic interpretation of nature, and some members of the scientific community have found confirmation of his teleological interpretation of nature.

Aristotle viewed the universe as a vast complex of organisms, with each organism trying to fulfill its nature. Organic structure is to be explained, then, by its function. The eye exists to see, the ear to hear, the whole body to live and perpetuate the species to which it belongs. But the key to all this lay in the subsequent, not the antecedent cause. Though the process of life may be described as evolutionary, it is not one of time. The human level of existence is not *later* than the inorganic level. The higher forms do not come *after* the lower ones. That is because all nature is a process of potentiality actualizing itself. Actuality is the realization of potentiality. It is more a pulling of nature than a pushing. For example, the oak is already in the acorn as potentiality, much as a house may be said to be already in the mind of the builder.

In the judgment of many scholars, the greatest achievement of Aristotle is his invention of logic, that eventually became the standard philosophical method. There is not another instance in mankind's entire intellectual history in which a single individual has brought into existence a new science, the influence of which is inestimable. For Aristotle logic was preparation for scientific knowledge, not knowledge itself. Because Aristotle himself viewed logic only as a tool, he gave it the name "organon." Aristotle was the first to analyze sentences, and he was the first to insist on rigorous scientific procedure, by use of the syllogism or by dialectic reasoning from the opinion of others. While his rules for argumentation are still taught in some quarters, they are discounted in others as proving nothing. Still, while deduction is not the most direct method at arriving at truth, it is helpful in preventing the reasoner from, drawing wrong conclusions.

It is in his reaction to Plato's theories of ethics, politics, and art that Aristotle's departure from his old master is most apparent. The *Ethics* and the *Politics* do not develop separate or independent subject matter. Aristotle, like Plato, would not adopt one method for ethics and another for politics. The difference between the *Ethics* and the *Politics* is that the one is concerned with the character of the individual and the other with the constitution of the state.

How good is Aristotle's *Ethics*? He missed much, admittedly, because his approach is psychological, and there was much about human behavior that Aristotle did not understand. But, on the other hand, the influence of the *Ethics* is incontestable. As has been frequently noted, there is something good on every page, and what he had to say on some matters can hardly be improved upon. If Aristotle does not know why people act the way they do, it is claimed, he at least knows how they act.

In his *Ethics*, Aristotle abandons Plato's idea that rests on the notion of absolute good. He is content to base theory on observable facts. Human good turns out to be activity of the soul in accordance with virtue. Moral principles, argues Aristotle, are not inborn as Socrates and Plato had maintained, nor are they artificial and conventional, as the sophists had taught. They are developed.

Socrates had taught that vice is involuntary; but Aristotle believed that, if that were so, virtue is also involuntary, and as little deserving of praise as vice is of blame. For virtue is conformity with right desire, and reason is sufficient to teach us what that is. Our actions, he says, are like children—they should be conceived with dignity. This applies much to man as a moral agent as to man as a citizen.

In the *Politics*, Aristotle attacks almost every position set forth by Plato in the *Republic*. He is particularly in disagreement with Plato's rigidity in the application of authority, and with the role of government which favors a special class like the guardians. He favors instead flexibility, division of labor, and a variety of interests. He intensely dislikes Plato's communizing women, children, and property for the guardian class. What belongs to everyone, he says, belongs to no one, and thus will be neglected. Besides, in Plato's State, there is intolerable contact, with no room for privacy. Anyhow, Aristotle thinks men are too jealous to share their wives, and women are too maternal to give up their children. Besides, the family is a source of virtue needed by the state; it is a nurse of morals.

As for education, says Aristotle, to place the emphasis of education on professional training, as Plato does, is the mark of an illiberal mind. "To be always seeking after the useful does not become a free and exalted soul."

Aristotle differed with Plato, too, regarding the best form of government; whereas Plato preferred Aristocracy, Aristotle favors "polity"—a mean between oligarchy and democracy. Under such a government, the large middle class holds a balance between the upper class and the proletariat. The exercise of the vote and military service is restricted to property owners.

Aristotle's *Poetics* is the single most influential work ever written on literary criticism. It deals mainly with literary genres of tragedy and epic and its great influence was partly due to misunderstanding Aristotle's meaning. It was and is a mistake to read into Aristotle the doctrine of the three dramatic unities—time, place, and action. The last is the only one upon which he strictly insists. Perhaps no literary judgment has produced more controversy than Aristotle's remark that tragedy by raising pity and fear purges the mind of those emotions. This seemed to be Aristotle's way of responding to Plato's theory (expressed in the *Republic*) that tragedy is an incentive and stimulus to mischievous emotions.

But Aristotle's discussions about art go far beyond the nature of tragedy. In the matter of art as in the matter of ethics and politics, Aristotle takes issue with much of what Plato had to say. He agrees that the fine arts are imitative in and of nature, but imitation is not of the sensible world. Though the medium is sensuous, art is an expression of nature in a universal sense—as nature is revealed in the particular.

Moreover, art is not intended, as Plato had said, to teach morality. Only inferior audiences demand that art teach a lesson, by showing virtue triumphing over vice. The purpose of art is to give pleasure, and art is good to the extent it does so.

In addition, art is not to be condemned, as Plato had insisted, for arousing the emotions. This instead of harming the soul, purges and heals it.

Nor can it be said that art should give us esthetic expressions of the more elevated kind. Great art may do this, but man's other needs must be met as well. Art, then, has more to do with esthetics than with morality. If moral subjects are chosen for art, they must be esthetically pleasing. If not, art remains photographic and mediocre.

Aristotle would not permit art to be judged by a person with narrow interests—even by the artist himself. It is not for the cook to pass judgment on the food he has prepared, nor the maker of the rudder to judge how well it functions. Such judgments must be left to those for whom such things are intended. Aristotle is naturally led from such views to the position that the classics should not be censored. A subject of obvious ethical inferiority may be esthetically pleasing, and what seems unsatisfactory in part may be quite satisfying as a whole. But the artist should depict moral evil only when it contributes to the value of the whole work.

The influence of these best known treatises—the *Ethics*, the *Politics*, and the *Poetics*—remains strong even at the dawn of the twenty-first century, more than twenty-three hundred years after Aristotle wrote them. Some of his works are still used as textbooks in schools the world over. He was a teacher who inspired his students and was rewarded with their loyalty. Generations of pupils are still awed by the sheer magnitude of his achievements. The image of him bestriding antiquity like an intellectual colossus is appropriate praise for this passionate advocate of human reason.

With Aristotle, Greek philosophy achieved full and perfect maturity; but with his death it began a continuous decline. In fact, many of the Greeks of the Hellenistic period were not even capable of understanding Aristotle's metaphysics because they lacked the ability to grasp the philosophical problems in the profound manner in which Aristotle stated them. Subsequent thinkers, lacking Aristotle's originality, simply copied the opinions of Plato and Aristotle. Metaphysical inquiry was neglected. The times called for more practical concerns. Thus the Hellenic thought becomes less searching and profound in the hands of the moralists who, after Aristotle's time, fill the Hellenic cities and later the cities of the Roman Empire. In our own time, many of Aristotle's ideas have been appropriated by thinkers who are scarcely aware of the extent of their indebtedness.

Because Aristotle's work ranged over several branches of philosophy and laid the foundation of many of them, his main themes and ideas have never been out of fashion, although he has been more highly regarded in some periods than in others. His ideas have stimulated philosophers for centuries precisely because they can be interpreted meaningfully in various ways. Aristotle retains the interest of modern philosophers because the problems he struggled so hard to make clear are still unresolved. Moreover many of our best known philosophical methods are those he invented or made popular. His achievements are better understood and appreciated now than ever before, since his ideas are embedded in the subjects he examined with such meticulous care. Wherever he placed his hand, he left the imprint of his unique and universal genius.

No other thinker has built into his system such a staggering collection of facts. Because Aristotle's philosophy brought existing knowledge within a single focus, it is perhaps the most comprehensive, and creative synthesis of knowledge ever produced by a single individual, and it stands as one of the supreme achievements of the mind of man. It is a feat no one before him had attempted, and few after him have matched. By integrating such concepts as substance, matter and form, actuality and potentiality, etc., he set forth the fundamental concepts of science and philosophy which were to last from his day to ours. His work laid the foundation for all later histories of Greek thought, and the ideal of human excellence he established remains undiminished.

DA VINCI

BY
JERRY
ANDERSON

# Leonardo da Vinci
## 1452-1519

*"Whatever exists in the universe, in essence, in appearance, in the imagination, the painter has first in his mind and then in his hands; and these are of such excellence that they are able to present a proportioned and harmonious view of the whole that can be seen simultaneously, at one glance, just as things in nature."*

It is one thing to say of a man that he is a genius. It is quite another thing to say of him that he is perhaps the most versatile genius that ever lived. The reference to Leonardo's versatility includes much more than his many-sidedness. That was a characteristic quite common in Leonardo's time, an identifiable feature of the "Renaissance Man." Leonardo's genius included his ability to retain his popularity through the centuries, appealing to diverse tastes.

For almost three centuries Leonardo was appreciated primarily as an artist. (In fact, among all the artist-scientists of the Renaissance, Leonardo best deserves that title.) His notebooks containing his remarkable understanding of mechanics were not widely known in his lifetime, and some were discovered as recently as 1965. When the first edition of the notebooks appeared in 1881, the world was introduced to a Leonardo it had never known—Leonardo the scientist.

But even without this latest evidence of his genius, his reputation was secure. The most distinguished writers in Europe—Göethe, Wordsworth, Rossetti, Pater, Shelly, Stendhal, Baudelaire, to mention only a few in the span of one hundred years—poured out their praise in poetry and prose; and the features of his art which inspired this outpouring of adulation seemed inexhaustible.

The mystery in all this is how so much could be written about a man whose personal life remains largely hidden from public view. Surprisingly enough Leonardo is treated now as often as a scientist as an artist. That is partly because his work as a scientist has come to light only recently and partly because the scope of it is so breathtaking. It literally defies the last word. But then, so, apparently, does his painting. There has never been a time when his works have not been considered masterpieces in one country or another.

Leonardo was an extremely complex character as well. The first to see the universal source of knowledge in nature, he explored all fields of human knowledge, inserting his superb intellect into every realm where graphic representation is employed—painting, sculpture, architecture, and engineering. Not only did he master the art of drawing, but he possessed an exceptional grasp of anatomy, astronomy, botany, zoology, hydrodynamics and music. And any attempt to capture his genius must include his forays into physiology, optics, geology, geography, meteorology, aeronautics, physics, phonetics, linguistics, and mathematics. He drew up plans for hundreds of inventions, including an airplane and a parachute. It seems not, then, too much to claim that Leonardo was the most energetic, versatile, and inclusive genius that humanity has so far produced.

But it was not just the praise of posterity that earned him fame. He drew an outpouring of admiration from his contemporaries, much of it directed toward his character and physical attributes, as well as toward his art. Vasari, in his *Lives of the Painters*, records that the Duke of Milan, "hearing Leonardo's marvelous discourses became so enamored of his qualities that it appeared incredible." Referring to the period of the artist's youth, he says, "With his reasoning he conquered and with his arguments he confounded every strong intellect," and adds, "He was so pleasing in conversation that he drew to himself people's very hearts." Vasari's own admiration was so great that he included him among those who "represent not only humanity but also divinity itself."

Benevuto Cellini, reflecting on Leonardo's genius concerning "the three great arts of sculpture, painting, and architecture," exclaims, " ...

No greater man then he, I believe, has been born into the world." Cellini then quotes the words spoken to him by King Francis I, of France, that he believed "no other man had been born into the world who knew as much as Leonardo—not so much speaking of sculpture, painting, and architecture, as saying that he was a very great philosopher."

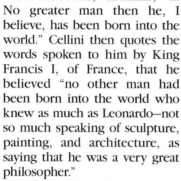

What philosophy Leonardo dispensed was broadly conceived, but not so focused as to found a school, as his painting did. Some of his most impressive utterances have to do with his precepts for living, and only a few examples are required to show the nature of his thought. His advice to those who pursue art and understanding is sound: "Avoid that study the resultant work of which dies with the worker." "It is wrong for you to praise and worse to reprehend a thing if you do not understand it well." "The acquisition of any knowledge is always of use to the intellect, because it may drive out useless things and preserve the good. For nothing can be loved or hated unless it is first understood."

But it is in the field of ethics that Leonardo most strongly reveals the nobility of his character:

"Knowledge acquired in one's youth arrests the damage of old age, and if you understand that old age has wisdom for its sustenance, you will so conduct yourself in youth that your old age will not lack nourishment."

"And you, O man, who will observe in these things I have made the wonderful works of nature, if you think it would be a criminal thing to destroy these, consider how much more criminal it is to take the life of a man. And if this, his external form, appears to you marvelously constructed, remember that it is nothing as compared with the soul that dwells in that structure; for that, indeed, be it what it may, is a thing divine. Leave it then to dwell in its function at its pleasure, and let not your rage or malice destroy a life—for truly, he who does not value life does not himself deserve it."

Leonardo was an illegitimate son of a man who made his living as a notary and of a peasant woman. She married an artisan in the region of Vinci, near Florence, shortly after Leonardo's birth. Leonardo was twenty-four before his father had another child (by his third or fourth wife); and though he grew up in a childless household, he was treated as though he were a legitimate child. Leonardo did not receive a humanistic education, but was given the elementary education available to about a third of the children in the province. As a result, he got little instruction in mathematics and in Latin—a deficiency of which he was always keenly aware and strove to overcome.

About 1467, then a boy of fifteen, he was apprenticed to the painter and sculptor Andrea del Verrochio, in whose workshop he learned the value of careful observation and diversified workmanship; and it was probably here that Leonardo began to develop the many-sided aspect of his genius. Vasari described Verrochio as "goldsmith, master of perspective, sculptor, painter, musician." In 1472 Leonardo was admitted to the painters' guild of Florence after five years of training. He remained with Verrochio for another five years and then opened his own workshop in Florence.

A review of Leonardo's migratory life would suggest that he was a man without a "country." While Italy was, in Leonardo's time, a collection of city-states and remained so until the nineteenth century, he claimed no allegiance to any city, and moved freely between them. Born in Florence in 1452, Leonardo spent the first thirty years of his life there before finding work in Milan. From 1482 to 1499, he worked on various projects in Milan—including painting, sculpture, and architecture—but never completed many of these. In 1600 he returned to Florence for six years (by way of Mantua and Venice), and then made his way back to Milan in 1506 for another six years, with a brief six-months' return to Florence during 1507-1508. In 1513 he went to Rome for a period of three years, finally leaving Italy for good in 1516, to serve in the court of King Francis I of France. And there he died three years later, in 1519.

Continuous references have been made over the centuries to the "disdainful aloofness" of Leonardo, to his loneliness, to his penchant for solitude, to his sometimes harsh and condemnatory rhetoric. His secret estrangement has remained a mystery. He, like the objects in nature he sought to understand, has been analyzed and psychoanalyzed by the best of minds—including Sigmund Freud's. In a "half-fictional" work published in 1910, Freud sought the answer to this enigmatic personality in Leonardo's childhood. But Freud was explaining only one aspect of Leonardo's personality, derived from an incident in Leonardo's youth. A young man of seventeen was accused of having a homosexual affair with four other youths from the city of Florence, one of whom was Leonardo.

Such charges were not uncommon in Florence in the fifteenth century. They seemed, indeed, to be almost invited. By means of a *tamburo*, a box placed outside the Palazzo Vecchio, secret charges could be made against anyone in the city, charges which the "vice squad" could investigate. Leonardo was called before the police and cruelly interrogated until, one imagines, his soul was laid quite bare; then, after a few weeks of no further action, the charges were dropped.

But one might suppose that Leonardo never saw the world in the same way after that excruciating experience. While he may have exhibited an androgynous nature in his art, it is perhaps because he saw the world in all its complicated relatedness. But, it is claimed, he never saw men or women as sex objects, judging by the written testimony of his own hand, or the sex act as anything but disgusting. Even after the passing of many years he was to write, "The act of coitus and the members that serve it are so hideous that, if it were not for the beauty of faces and craftsmen ornamentation and the liberation of the spirit, the human species would lose its humanity."

There is no evidence to suggest that Leonardo had a woman in his life in any intimate way, no female companions, no one to smile on him or offer words of encouragement. By his own admission, he preferred it that way: "So that prosperity of the body may not ruin prosperity of the mind, the painter must live solitary. Alone, you are all yourself; with a companion you are half yourself. And so you squander yourself according to the indiscretion of your

company." Leonardo always had someone around him, often very young apprentices, as he himself once was, or older men assisting with some unrealized project. Still, there was always an anti social element in Leonardo, and he retained a certain aloofness and haughtiness to the very end.

The Renaissance sought to affirm the healthier version of the Greek idea of sexless love, which is the kind Leonardo seems to have chosen. And this Greek ideal—at least in Athens—which had been "softened in Alexandria, coarsened in Rome, and damned by Christianity," re-emerged in Florence with vigor and passion.

If Leonardo took as his apprentices slim, handsome boys, what of that? He himself had been one in Verrochio's workshop. Besides, they were needed to pose for the religious figures they represented, such as David. If Leonardo was thought to be "strangely beautiful," that was hardly his fault. Moreover, there is no evidence that Leonardo himself was overcome by Platonic love as was, for example, Michelangelo, who gave himself over to it with the enthusiasm that exceeded that of Dante or Petrarch. Yet, so little is known of Leonardo's personal life that it is dangerous to push any theory too far—a fact even Freud recognized.

Anyhow, the "beauty of faces" referred to by Leonardo in his morose reference to sex is how the world first came to know him. In his "Baptism of Christ," painted in collaboration with Verrochio in 1472, Leonardo depicts the "beauty of faces" in a way that has hardly been surpassed. Throughout his career as a painter, he continued to paint face after face of exquisite beauty. Leonardo once claimed that the painter has two chief things to paint—man and the contents of his mind. But whatever subject was selected, it must come from nature, and be governed by the same laws that govern nature.

Of Leonardo's paintings, only about ten that are certifiably his exist. Another half a dozen are in dispute. What his paintings have in common is their breathtaking beauty. It could be seen as early as his "Baptism of Christ," and his "Adoration of the Magi," completed just before he entered the service of the Duke of Milan in 1482. His first version of the "Virgin of the Rocks" was finished soon after his arrival in Milan, and "The Last Supper" just a couple of years before he left that city. The "Mona Lisa" (sometimes called "La Giaconda") was painted in 1503, after his return to Florence. The "Madonna with St. Anne" was painted during his second stay in Milan, and "St. John the Baptist," a product of his brief stay in Rome, was painted in 1515. The "Mona Lisa" and "The Last Supper" are among the most popular paintings ever produced by human hand.

In all of this art, Leonardo shows himself to be a master of the High Renaissance style, with his original studies in light and shade, in paying less attention to accessory detail, and in the more generalized statement made by establishing clear, logical relationships among the objects of the painting. Still, many of his paintings were not given the final touch of his brush. (The "Battle of Anghiari," like "The Last Supper," was painted in an experimental medium, and the colors ran soon after they were applied. Nothing of it remains. It, along with a painting by Michelangelo, was destined for the Hall of the Great Council in the Palazzio Vecchio.) The conceptualization of projects was always more fruitful for Leonardo than their execution. In the last years of his life, he turned exclusively to drawing, believing it to be the basic form of art because it alone can reflect the essence of things. Moreover, he lost interest in the use of color in art, because he considered it both external and superficial. Still the school of painting inspired by Leonardo is considered more important than that of any other artist at any time, and it includes at least forty five painters, including Raphael, Rubens, and Michelangelo.

In sculpture, too, Leonardo, often left works unrealized. Leonardo is thought to have studied sculpture in Verrochio's studio. Some minor pieces of sculpture are mentioned by Vasari, his first biographer, but nothing by Leonardo remains. Although Leonardo had written in his *Treatise on Painting* that sculpture is a "lesser genius than painting," he goes on to point out

that he has worked "no less in sculpture than in painting, being equally adept at the one and the other." Two of his grandly conceived monuments were not completed. "The Horse" (a monument in memory of Francesco Sforza) was to be twenty feet high and require 20,000 pounds of bronze. The bronze was diverted to making cannons, and the French used the life-size clay model for target practice. His second project, a tomb sculpture for Trivulsio, did not get even so far as a clay model. Still, his reputation was great enough to win him appointment to the committee established to select an appropriate location in Florence for Michelangelo's "David."

Leonardo's work in architecture also had a lack of finality about it. Although he had a life-long interest in architecture, and was at one time in competition with Bramante, the architect of St. Peter's in Rome, his work was confined by chance or by choice to that of an advisor; but his brilliance in architecture is reflected in his surviving sketches.

During his first Milan years, in the 1480's and 1490's, Leonardo began his "Notebooks," on which pages were recorded his astonishing drawings of a scientific nature—the anatomy of the human body, plans for machines, fortifications, canals, etc.—accompanied by careful notation. Leonardo was left-handed, and he wrote in a right-to-left script that can be read with a mirror. He kept a small pad of paper on his belt, or in his pocket, on which he scribbled tentative ideas which were later transferred to larger sheets of paper. Thousands of these sheets survive. Many were combined into "notebooks," of which thirty-one have been identified. Taken together, they constitute one of the most remarkable collections ever penned by a single individual; and they reveal Leonardo's intellectual interest in every field of inquiry open to him.

Leonardo's interest was not just in subjects suitable for painting, but in every object to which the laws of nature pertained, the most important of which was man. He viewed man as the embodiment of the physical universe. Man, for Leonardo, was something of a miracle; the human body, something divine.

The body, as Leonardo envisioned it, required a life-giving source and a life-preserving force. Leonardo was content to draw upon Aristotelian sciences for that, believing, as most people in his day still believed, that this cosmic force of the universe is located in the soul and is in turn capable of being transmitted to other organs of the body. Everywhere Leonardo looked he saw force at work. Primal mechanical forces were to be seen not only in gravitation, energy, and momentum, but in the flight of birds, in the movement of water and of air, in the growth of plants and animals, in the flame of a candle, in smoke and in clouds. It is in the analysis of this force that Leonardo displays his incomparable ingenuity. And he displays, too, his ability to assemble the disparate elements of his knowledge under a guiding principle: nature is subject to law—a law of necessity and order without which all would be chaos.

"Force, I define," says Leonardo "as a spiritual

power, incorporeal or invisible which with brief life is produced in those bodies which as the result of accidental violence are brought out of their natural state and condition." But, then, considering that Leonardo saw this force as clearly in the waves of a woman's hair as in the waves of the water or the currents of the air, it became evident that it would be extremely difficult to separate Leonardo the scientist from Leonardo the painter—because, in sketching these various phenomena, his hand moved in the same way.

To see how readily Leonardo mixes art and science one need only review his ideas about their relationship, because for him art and science were not two separate things. He saw himself first and foremost as a painter in search of knowledge, of understanding. But that can be had only with the eye which "knows how to see," of the hand which "knows how to follow the intellect." Art, then, is ultimately an experience of the intellect; and it is the work of the hand which defines the compass of man's thought.

It is instructive to trace in Leonardo's own words the primacy of the sense of sight: "Now do you not see that the eye embraces the beauty of the whole? It is the lord of astronomy and the maker of cosmography; it counsels and corrects all the arts of mankind; it leads men to different parts of the world; it is the prince of mathematics, and the sciences founded on it are absolutely certain. It has measured the distances and sizes of the stars; it has found the elements and their locations; it divines the future from the course of the stars; it has given birth to architecture, and to perspective, and to the divine art of painting."

The idea that the senses could yield the truth about nature would have come as news to most of Leonardo's contemporaries, who still clung to the authority of the scholastic tradition. But for Leonardo, experience was more important than authority. "Anyone who argues by referring to authority," he writes, "is not using his mind but rather his memory." That is why he broke from the philosophy of the schools that believed not only that reality can be mirrored but that it can be captured in a web of words. "Necessity," wrote Leonardo, "constrains the mind of the painter to transmute itself into nature's own mind, and to make itself an interpreter between nature and art." The artist thus becomes a transmitter of the data of experience, and he alone is pre-eminently qualified to probe and unfold the secrets of nature.

On this view, art is the road man takes to knowledge, and, eventually, to action. In a Platonic sense, this process becomes an act of love—"the union with the thing that is known." The act is essentially creative, because the knowledge of nature gleaned from observation makes it possible for man to overcome his limitations and learn a new power over nature. As it was acknowledged by Renaissance thinkers that God revealed himself in nature, it was natural to seek Him there. It was, in fact, a religious expression to do so.

It is not, however, in his words but in his hundreds of drawings of machines, many of them his own inventions, that Leonardo revealed himself so stunningly as a scientist. Leonardo's scientific insights, no less than Galileo's, were a result of theories advanced by the Greeks, the Arabs, the medieval scholars Albert of Saxony, John Buridan, and others who were uncomfortable with Aristotle's principles. Aristotle believed that if force is not continually exerted on a body it will slow down and cease to move. But what applies to bodies subjected to obstruction of the medium they exist in is not true of celestial bodies, a fact that Aristotle did not recognize.

Now, in what sense can Leonardo be said to anticipate Galileo and others who were to work out a whole new theory of mechanics? In regard to the principles of motion, Leonardo made monumental contributions. "Every motion," says Leonardo, "tends to maintain itself, that is, every body that is moved always moves as long as the impression of the motive forces remains in it." In another place, he writes, "Every body will follow its path in a straight line as long as the violence done by its motive force persists in it." The principle of inertia—the tendency to persist in a straight line or at rest—is apparent in these passages, although complicated somewhat by the "impetus theory" of the fourteenth century scholars in Paris and London. Also reminiscent of Galileo are some of the properties of an enclosed plane discovered by Leonardo. Apart from his anticipation of Galileo, there is an anticipation of Newton in Leonardo's principle of reaction: "An object offers as much resistance to the air as the air offers to the object." "Every body goes in a direction opposite to the place from which it is driven by the object that strikes it ..." In other words, an action is equal to and contrary to the reaction. Leonardo, it may be concluded, clearly had an understanding of the first and third laws of motion.

To appreciate even more fully Leonardo's contribution to science, one can look at his work on the impact of elastic and inelastic bodies, his work on the propelling action of the screw, his understanding of the principle of the syphon, of communicating vessels, of the parachute, of the inverted images obtained by a convergent lens and rectified by another lens. The list seems endless. Even in the science of anatomy, Leonardo's competency was so certain that, had he continued his studies, he almost certainly would have arrived at the conclusions reached by Vesalius and Harvey.

Much of Leonardo's fondness for experimental science was put to work as a military engineer, which involved his competency as a hydraulic engineer. His studies in military art and architecture and the mechanics and technology to support it were pursued while he was still in Florence. In 1503 he was serving as a military engineer for the city of Florence. Along with Machiavelli, he worked on his plan to divert the Arno River, so that Pisa would be cut off from traffic with the sea and be forced to surrender.

Before departing from Milan in 1482, to enter the service of Ludovico, the Duke of Milan, Leonardo composed a letter outlining his qualifications. He mentions portable bridges, scaling

ladders, means of cutting off water from trenches during a siege, methods of destroying fortresses; he mentions mortars, gunpowder, cannon-resistant ships, means of moving forces by traveling underneath enemy trenches or underneath a river; he mentions chariots armed with artillery [tanks]; and he mentions his knowledge of cannons, and, light ordnance. Yet, while Leonardo made significant contributions to military hardware and tactics, war always remained for him "a most beastly madness."

As Leonardo's competence in mathematics grew, so did his competency in scientific subjects. In the first decade of the sixteenth century, he intensified his studies in mathematics, even beginning a notebook on the geometry of solids. Thinkers like Leonardo became convinced that the key of the universe was to be found in mathematical proportion. That is why Leonardo could speak of mechanics as "the paradise of the mathematical sciences, because in it we come to the fruit of mathematics," and it is why he could say, "There is no certainty as to where one of the mathematical sciences cannot

be applied, nor as to where mathematics is not connected with them." "No human inquiry," he wrote, "can be called true science unless it passes through mathematical demonstrations." Leonardo's contributions to science, while generally unknown, are incontestable. It is almost impossible to measure their magnitude, but his approach to science was always as an artist.

Leonardo's desire to know the form and function of everything that existed found its most forceful expression in his drawings of the human body. The classical studies of the human body carried out by the Greeks and Romans, with their emphasis on life-like representation and an unabashed appreciation of beauty, had been long abandoned in Leonardo's time. Religious and mystical meaning was substituted, and pre-Renaissance painters like Cimabue, antedating Giotto and Botticelli, worked under the restrictions imposed on painters by the Roman Catholic Church. Sculptured human forms were regarded as "graven images," and any representation of the human body as fleshly substance was considered sinful. As a result, painters were constrained to present their subjects as two-dimensional, flat and unrealistic.

The Renaissance provided new ways for experiencing thought and feeling and encouraged artists to study nature more directly, more classically; and that led, eventually, to a scientific analysis of the human body. Leonardo began his study of anatomy to lend realism to his painting, but soon he approached it as a means of informing the intellect which underlies all art. Thus, Leonardo launched the first scientific study of the human body, providing a detailed reproduction of the body and its organs. Beginning with the skeleton and muscles, he progressed to the internal organs—particularly the brain, heart, and lungs. He developed a method for revealing hidden parts when viewed graphically by a layering or "hatching" process. His "picture chart" of the body laid out the principles which are employed in modern scientific illustrations.

In Leonardo's time anatomy was a fledgling art, with few skillful practitioners. By his own count, Leonardo dissected in his lifetime thirty corpses, on dissecting tables in Milan and a hospital in Florence. The literally hundreds of drawings that survive give vivid testimony to how well Leonardo learned his craft. It was for him a lifelong interest; but he never regarded it as an end in itself, obviously, because while his drawings are anatomically correct, his paintings are not.

While he introduced the feeling of geometric proportion into his paintings by means of curved and straight lines, he did not insist upon anatomical accuracy. And the reason for that might be that he recognized the need to achieve harmony in art by synthesizing its many disparate elements. But though his demand for realism was not purchased at the expense of his idealism, he never lost his desire to generalize by means of mathematical and geometrical relationships.

Gabriel Séailles finds Leonardo to be cerebral in all he undertook. "For sentiment he substituted the idea, for unity of sentiment logical succession, for poetry science." He was perceived by his contemporaries as "the master of truth" because of all men then living he was best able to give a rational explanation for everything that he observed. Had circumstances favored him, he probably would have edited all his thousands of notes, completed all the treatises he had planned to write, and produced the world's first encyclopedia.

Perhaps one reason Leonardo did not finish everything he undertook is that he was always dissatisfied with what he had done. Another reason, probably, is that, because everything in nature interested him, he was constantly making drawings of and observations on objects of every kind. Besides, there were distractions of a mathematical nature, and investigations into the mysteries of science to claim his attention. And he continued to make forays into sculpture and architecture.

Leonardo viewed art as something that must be surpassed: "It is a sorry disciple that does not go beyond his master." But the master (knowing what art is) cannot help feel sadness when he sees his work falling short of his ideal: "It is a sorry master whose work surpasses his judgment; and the master tends towards the perfection of art whose work is surpassed by his judgment."

Sometimes Leonardo's distractions from painting occupied long stretches of time, which drew a deprecating remark from Castiglione: "Another of the greatest painters in the world despises that art in which he is so rare: he sets himself to studying philosophy, from which he derives such strange concepts and novel chimeras that with all his crafts he would not be able to paint them."

Just being in Rome during 1513 to 1516—those years when the city was being transformed by the feverish work of some of the greatest painters, sculptors, and architects in history—should have been exciting enough for anyone. Bramante was building St. Peter's, Michelangelo had just completed the Sistine Ceiling, and Raphael was decorating the papal apartments. But whatever sense of excitement Leonardo had upon entering Rome soon vanished. He painted very little in Rome and nothing during his years in France, from 1516-1519.

When he left Rome to serve as court painter for King Francis I of France, he took his favorite student (the young nobleman Melzi), a servant, and two of his paintings—the "Mona Lisa" and "St John,"—which he could never bring himself to part with. The "Mona Lisa" was not, apparently, commissioned by the young girl's husband; and both paintings contained elements which for Leonardo represented spiritual as well as strictly representational meaning. As with his other works, Leonardo did not consider them finished; and he never finished them. While in France he suffered from some paralysis of his left arm, which made it necessary to shift much of the responsibility for what he did attempt onto Melzi.

He died in the company of Melzi and his servant, no longer a man who contemplated subjugating nature, and content to turn to the Church for what solace it could give, asking God to forgive him for not using all the resources of his spirit and his art.

Many were quick to note that "wherever he turned his thoughts, mind, and spirit, he showed such sublimity in everything that for perfection in quickness, vivacity, goodness, grace, and charm, no one has ever equalled him." Those who knew him praised him for his patience, forgiveness, and manly acceptance of work. "Death before weariness," he had written. "No work shall tire me. I do not grow weary of serving." And, as a sort of afterthought, he adds, "A life well spent is long. Just as the day well spent gives grateful sleep, so a life well employed gives grateful death."

To those of us who are the beneficiaries of his remarkable life, accounts of his death evoke no strong emotions. Yet, in an age when many sidedness was not rare, there emerged a man who was truly a citizen of the world, a "universal man," displaying a genius that goes beyond boundaries and national sentiment. Just as his contemporaries recognized in his artistic genius a diversity expressive of the humanist ideal of Renaissance Italy, a more skeptical, practical generation like ours still can discover in Leonardo a quality that transcends everyday, earthbound experiences, and gives wings to the imagination.

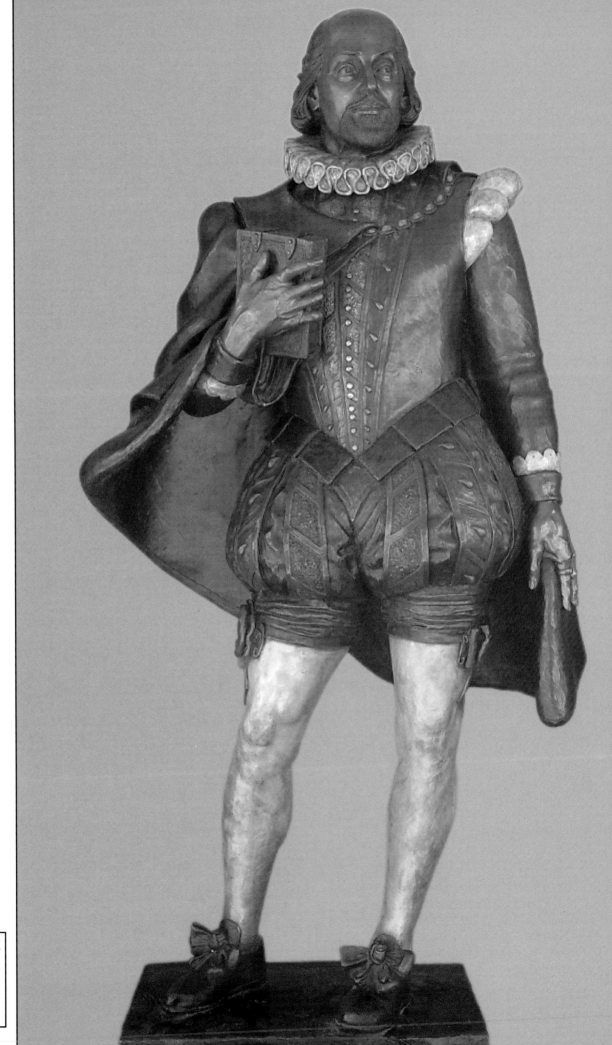

SHAKESPEARE

BY
JERRY
ANDERSON

# William Shakespeare
## 1564-1616

> "*Sure, he that made us with such large discourse,*
> *Looking before and after, gave us not,*
> *That capability and godlike reason*
> *To fust in us unused.*"

The world has many respected writers, but none is held in such high esteem and affection as is William Shakespeare—one of the few writers who has been embraced by the entire world. He has been compared to the apostle Paul in his internationalism; but while Paul set out to spread Christ's message to a skeptical world and had great influence on the Mediterranean world in his lifetime, Shakespeare's interests were confined to his beloved England, and his influence did not extend beyond a theater-loving London in his lifetime. And, while it may be true that Shakespeare fulfills the poet's task the way Wordsworth defined it of "binding together by passion and knowledge the empire of human society, as it is spread over the whole earth and over all time," there is little evidence to suggest that Shakespeare realized that this is what he was doing.

It is almost impossible to refer to William Shakespeare in anything but superlatives. He is undoubtedly the most popular author the world has known. His greatness is a result of his remarkably unique creative talents in drama and in poetry. The reputation that Shakespeare enjoys today as a writer of unparalled ability was not the one he enjoyed in his own lifetime. He was attacked from time to time by his contemporaries, but he was an extremely popular playwright, as demonstrated by the number of times his plays were performed, by the frequency with which his name was used to market writing he had little or no part in, and by the large amount of wealth he amassed by his profession.

It was largely because of his talent as a dramatist that Shakespeare was able to make a living writing for the stage. Few other writers of his time were able to do so. By the late 1590's he was an established dramatist, and yet he had not written any of the tragedies that are considered his crowning work—*Hamlet*, *Othello*, *King Lear*, and *Macbeth*. While many scholars believe that *King Lear* is Shakespeare's greatest work, the most popular of the four, *Hamlet*, has given us more proverbial expressions than any other work by a single author. It was he who gave us such idioms as "fair play," "foregone conclusion," "catch cold," "disgraceful conduct," "in one fell swoop," and "that's the rub." And he is thought to have invented such words as "assassination," "bump," "eventful," and "lonely." Shakespeare and his contemporaries treated English as a dynamic, versatile language rather than as one confined by rules. Of course, English has always been a dynamic language. While the "father of English poetry," Geoffrey Chaucer, had 8,000 words in his vocabulary, Shakespeare, two hundred years later, had 24,000 words in his.

But, of all the writers of his time, Shakespeare was the most successful in creating vivid images through the use of language by applying varied stylistic techniques. He employed "image clusters" frequently in his plays, allowing one image to call forth several others, not necessarily related. Like all Elizabethan writers, his training in rhetoric led him to use elaborate, structured language full of conceits, puns, and double meanings.

It is no mystery that Shakespeare is so often

quoted. He had a great deal to say on an unlimited supply of subjects, and he said it in an incomparably memorable way. It is not only the melodic lilt of his verses that charms us, but the natural gaiety that finds its way into so much of what he has written. So pervasive is his influence that his writings have helped shape the culture as well as the literature of many countries, including that of Russia and Germany.

But as much as his language, his skill as a storyteller profoundly moves us. To carry the action of his masterly constructed plots, he fills the stage with comic, tragic, and historical characters who capture our interest and engage our passions. Many of them have been scrutinized and analyzed as though they had a reality apart from the stage. So skillfully did Shakespeare employ his dramatic technique that his popularity came early and was widespread—and it has endured.

His popularity supports a publishing industry, an acting industry, a large community of scholars, and several commercial enterprises. His plays have inspired such motion pictures as *West Side Story, Kiss Me Kate,* and *The Boys from Syracuse*; such musical compositions as the *Otello* and *Falstaff of Verdi*; and a host of graphic art works.

Precious little is known of Shakespeare's life before the splenetic attack on him by a fellow actor in 1592; and, if it were not for some entries in the records of the parish church in Stratford-upon-Avon, nothing would be known. Church records show his baptism on April 26, 1564. Since baptisms were generally held three days after birth, it is assumed he was born on April 23. That date is significant because his monument records the date of his death in 1616 also as April 23. What also is recorded of him in the church records is his marriage when he was eighteen to Anne Hathaway, nine years his senior; the birth of a daughter six months later; and the birth of twins, a boy and a girl a couple of years after that. And that is it.

**E**verything else pertaining to his first twenty-eight years is conjecture, some almost certain, some merely speculative. For example, it is almost certain that he attended the local school which he could have done with no cost since his father was bailiff, or mayor.

There is a period of time from 1584 to 1592 referred to as "the missing years" because there is no knowledge of where he was located. Was he a school teacher? Was he a soldier in the low countries? Was he a servant in a wealthy household? No one knows. What is known is that there were three theatrical troupes playing in Stratford from 1583 to 1585, the latter being the year the twins were born, and he must have begun his work in the theater shortly after that. It is not likely that he ran off with a troupe as one might run off with a circus. He had a family, and what records exist show that he was a loving and a caring husband and father. But the theatrical performances in his home town may well have enticed him to seek a career in the theater in London.

London in Shakespeare's time was remarkably diverse in its thought and character, with a population of about 200,000 people. Queen Elizabeth was regarded as God's earthly representative, but religious belief was divided almost to the point of civil war. Elizabeth's father, Henry VIII, in 1534 broke from the Roman Catholic Church of England. Queen Mary established Catholicism as the state religion in 1553, but Elizabeth reestablished the Church of England in 1588. The wounds created by Henry VIII's act of defiance were deep and long-lasting. A Catholic uprising had occurred shortly before Shakespeare's arrival in London, and the new church was preaching against rebellion. Shakespeare's mother's family was Catholic, but his father was a member of the Church of England.

The lands once owned by the Catholic Church were being redistributed, education was being encouraged, money was flowing into London from the discovery of new lands. Puritanism had become firmly established by Luther and Calvin; Copernicus had challenged the heliocentric theory of the universe; Montaigne the theory that animals exist for man's pleasure and survival. And, only a couple of years after Shakespeare's arrival in London, in 1588, the English navy defeated the mighty Spanish Armada. It was an exciting time to be in London.

When Shakespeare arrived in London, the theater was not exactly in its infancy. It was, in a manner of speaking, about seven hundred years old. Its beginnings were in the "Trope" of the ninth century; this was followed by "Liturgical" plays leading to "Miracle plays," and eventually to "Morality plays" in the fifteenth century; and about the beginning of the sixteenth century, the "Interlude," a brief semi-dramatic comedy with coarse and farcical humor, appeared. The drama as it was known in Shakespeare's time was strongly influenced by the tragedies of Seneca and the comedies of Plautus and Terence. This Roman influence was pervasive, and Shakespeare, like his predecessors and contemporaries—Lyly, Kyd, Greene, Peele, and Marlowe—made heavy use of it.

The Roman plays provided examples of dramatic elements which many writers attempted to make universal. Tragedy employed such techniques as division into five acts, the so-called unities of time, place, and action, the exclusion of comedy from tragedy, the practice of having action reported on stage rather than taking place there, the emphasis on character, the use of a chorus, and the employment of such stock devices as tyrant, confidant, and ghost. The Roman comedies provided examples of wit, of sententiousness, of well-constructed plots, and natural dialogue. Shakespeare rejected the practice of the unities, though he observed them in The *Comedy of Errors* and *The Tempest*. In addition to the plays based on the Roman playwrights, the translation of *Plutarch's Lives* into English by Thomas North gave Shakespeare a host of subjects for his Roman plays, such as *Julius Caesar*, and *Antony and Cleopatra*. In fact, some of his Roman plays render whole pages of North into verse.

Shakespeare's plays are loosely divided into comedies, tragedies, and histories. Shakespeare was to perfect the technique of writing tragedy and comedy, but it is with English history that he began. His sources were the chronicles of Edward Hall and Raphael Holinshed, which provided a wealth of information pertaining to Queen Elizabeth's royal predecessors.

Though chronicle plays were rare before 1590, from 1590 to 1600 they were the most popular plays performed in London, and every playwright turned to writing them. The reason for their popularity is not difficult to find. The defeat of the Spanish Armada resulted in rampant patriotism, with historians and poets celebrating England and its traditions.

Shakespeare's venture into history began with his first tetralogy (there was to be a second)—the three parts of *Henry VI* and *Richard III*. The lack of dramatic unity in *Henry VI* reveals a young dramatist still struggling with his craft. In *Richard III*, Marlowe's influence is still present; but then the play was written in the manner of Marlowe's *Tamburlaine* and *Edward II*, although the sources are Hall and Holinshed. With *Richard III*, Shakespeare can be seen strengthening his technique.

Shakespeare's early comedies are clearly the work of a man learning his craft; and though his first comedy, *The Comedy of Errors*, lacks originality and has some technical problems, it has been said that modern English comedy first sees the light in it. His first tragedy, on the other hand, *Titus Andronicus*, with its scenes of rape, mutilation, and cannibalism, repulses many critics who cannot believe that Shakespeare wrote it; but seen by an Elizabethan audience, it was sheer melodrama, a reworking of an old popular one. In adapting the play, he reduced ten acts to five, and demonstrated maturity in the handling of action and suspense.

By now, 1592, Shakespeare at age twenty-eight had served an apprenticeship in the theater, revealing a promise in all three dramatic genres—history, comedy, and tragedy. And in that year, his predecessor, the playwright and pamphleteer Robert Greene, displayed his peevish attitude toward Shakespeare in his infamous, condemnatory lines: "There is an upstart crow, beautified with our feathers, that with his *Tyger's heart wrapt in a Player's hide* supposes that he is as well able to bombast out a blank verse as the best of you; and being an absolute *Johannes fac totum* [Jack-of-all-trades], is in his own conceit the only Shakescene in a country." The remark makes fun of a line in *Henry VI*, part II: "O tiger's heart wrapt in a woman's hide."

The publisher of Greene's spiteful letter was quick to follow it up with an apology—in response to protests, no doubt—attesting to Shakespeare's honesty as a man and to his "grace in writing." Greene died soon after writing his attack.

As luck would have it, Shakespeare had no sooner tried his wings as a writer than the theaters were closed; and they remained closed until 1594, except for a few brief weeks. London had devastating visits of the plague, and had had for two hundred years. When the plague appeared, the commoners got the worst of it, and public gatherings were discouraged. But Shakespeare did not let his talents go undeveloped during this period. He turned to poetry.

Even the briefest treatment of Shakespeare must consider his role as a poet, a man living and writing in an age when poetry had achieved a valued and respected place in the sphere of human expression.

It is important to realize that drama is traditionally classified as a form of poetry. The classification usually run something like this: dramatic poetry, epic poetry, narrative poetry, lyric poetry, elegiac poetry, etc. Because the presence of poetry is not always found in drama, many scholars prefer to use the expression "poetic drama." By Shakespeare's time, the medium of the play traditionally included the use of blank verse (unrhymed iambic pentameter lines), with rhymed couplets rounding out a scene or act of a play. Thus, Shakespeare thought of drama as a splendid vehicle for poetry simply because it was. Still, the *Merry Wives of Windsor* is nearly all in prose, an unusual approach to the drama for Shakespeare.

Regarded in a manner that permits distinction, Shakespeare's poetry is expressed in two ways—internally, as songs in his plays, and externally, as independent, separately published poems. In the latter group are found his first deliberate and extended attempts as a poet, his *Venus and Adonis* (1593) and *The Rape of Lucrece* (1594). They were very popular in his lifetime with the reading public—which consisted of the literate and the wordly people of the day. The two narrative poems reveal Shakespeare's dexterity, if not his sincerity, as well as his vivid imagination and inventive use of the English language. They seem artificial only because they were composed in a conventional mode. It was the way writers then thought they were supposed to write.

Both poems rely on long elaborate and flowery speeches rather than on action for their effect. *Venus and Adonis* went through sixteen editions by 1640. *The Rape of Lucrece* by that date went through eight editions. Both poems were praised for their eloquent treatment of classical subjects, based on stories told by the Latin author Ovid. While *Venus and Adonis* is filled with erotic, sensual imagery, *The Rape of Lucrece* has not even the comedic element of the first poem to recommend it; to many it seems strarkly cold and distant.

Shakespeare dedicated both poems to Henry Wriothesley, the Third Earl of Southampton, a

young, wealthy, intelligent patron of the arts. That Shakespeare needed someone to advance his career as a writer is certain. When he arrived in London he had no social standing, no influence, no friends, and no money. As a result he required a rich and preferably noble patron who would be willing to repay Shakespeare's verses with his favors. Southampton must have appeared to Shakespeare to be the perfect patron. And Southampton must have taken immediately to the older Shakespeare (Southampton was only nineteen when Shakespeare dedicated the first poem to him). The two men became intimate friends.

The second example of Shakespeare's independent poems is his sonnet sequence of 154 sonnets, each containing fourteen lines. The sonnets are thought to have been written between 1593 and 1600. Although the sonnets can be arranged in loosely fitted groups, no suitable order for them has been discovered. Because there is no attempt to tell a story, there is nothing irrevocable about the sequence. What themes there are are intermittent. There is, however, an unrelenting emphasis on the imminence of death, with all that is associated with it—the destructive effect of time on beauty, vitality, and love; and the rapidity of physical decay. But it is not known whether the emotions expressed are genuine or merely conventionally acceptable.

The first 126 sonnets in the sequence were addressed to a young man and the next twenty-six sonnets rehearse the charms of what has come to be called the "dark lady," because she is described in the sonnets as a brunette. Some sonnets in the second group refer to a rival poet who is competing with the author for the lady's favors. Because the last two sonnets in the sequence have no identifiable connection to the others, many critics doubt that they were written by Shakespeare.

*W*hether he addressed Southampton in his sonnets, as is often assumed, is unknown. The sonnets were not published until 1609, a date ten or fifteen years after they were composed. Many of the sonnets, always popular, are considered to be among the world's finest poems. That at least some sonnets were in circulation during the 1590's is known from a reference to them in 1598 by Francis Meres, who in a survey of contemporary literature, makes mention of Shakespeare's "sugared sonnets among his private friends."

With the sonnets there appeared a poem titled *A Lover's Complaint*. That it was written by Shakespeare is questionable. Another poem of sixty-seven lines, *The Phoenix and the Turtle* (1600-1601), appeared in a work called *Love's Martyr*. The subject is platonic love, symbolized by two birds, the phoenix and the turtledove. The symbolism of the poem, together with its philosophical context and metaphysical language, has led critics to seek out biographical, political, and religious meanings.

It is quite natural that Shakespeare might

think of earning a reputation by his poetry—a reputation that was difficult to come by as a playwright. Shakespeare and other writers of his time did not expect to find lasting fame in play-writing. They looked to nondramatic poetry for that, as a more exalted form of communication.

A 383-year-old poem claimed to be by Shakespeare was discovered in 1981 in the Oxford University Library. It is titled *A Farewell Elegye in Memory of the late Virtuous Maister William Peeter*, and it treats of the death of a young actor in 1612, about the time Shakespeare retired from the theater. If genuine, it will have a bearing on how Shakespeare's other works are read, not only because of its form, but because of its content.

Some of Shakespeare's greatest lyrics are not found in his external poetry, but are found in the songs from the plays. They were often accompanied by music and are masterful expressions of the poet's art. Very few plays were without lyrics, and many admirers of Shakespeare think that *The Tempest* and *A Midsummer Night's Dream* are filled with songs from beginning to end.

The songs do not appear as mere decoration to the play, however, but have a dramatic purpose. They reflect the mood of the piece, or serve as a commentary on it, and are the result of the nature of the action and character being displayed. Sometimes they are used to clear the stage of its actors. They can carry tragedy, as in the case of Ophelia's mad songs; or they can suggest irrepressible laughter, as in the case of the romantic comedies, such as *As You Like It*. It is commonly agreed that of all the English dramatists who graced the English stage, none had more skill then Shakespeare in "sweetening his scenes" with songs. In Shakespeare, more than in any other dramatist, one finds the gaiety of the ballet (in the dancing songs), the solemnity of the motet, and the terse, witty expressions of the madrigal. Some of his songs were set to music in his own time by such notable composers as Thomas Morley and William Byrd.

When the theaters reopened in 1594, Shakespeare was ready to commit himself full time as a playwright. He was thirty years old, and, by now, he was quite sure of his ability to succeed. He was ready to move on to another phase of his life.

It is convenient to trace Shakespeare's career in the theater through "periods" because changes in his technique, circumstances, and in Shakespeare himself are quite pronounced. The first period, 1588 to 1596, was a time of experimentation. It was a period of apprenticeship;

and it revealed Shakespeare progressing from hired hand to actor, from actor to actor-adaptor, and from collaborator to a self-assured playwright. Histories, comedies, and tragedies were all attempted in this first period; all showed signs of, as yet, unrealized genius. And, by now, there probably was not much about human nature that Shakespeare did not know.

The second period, 1595 or 1596 to 1600, saw Shakespeare move out of the "workshop" into the world. The plays of this period were almost all comedies. They were rough, rollicking comedies; or refined joyous ones, but all gave evidence of his mastery of plot construction.

The third period, 1600-1608, revealed a marked change in the plays. It was the period of the great tragedies—*Hamlet*, *Othello*, *King Lear*, and *Macbeth*. But even the comedies, such as *Measure for Measure*, had changed. They had become somber even bitter in tone. Ghosts and witches have replaced the elves and fairies. His laughter has vanished. His wit has turned serious. But he was capable of revealing character in its highest expressions of passion and sympathy, and he was also capable of revealing the moral and spiritual dilemma of men and women; and because he was capable, he felt compelled to do so.

The fourth period, 1608 to 1611 or 13, was a period of final experimentation. Shakespeare moves from the dark comedies and the heavy tragedies to the more pleasant mood of comedy. But his comedy has changed from what it was in the second period. Shakespeare critics and scholars have identified this group as "romances." *The Tempest* is the most notable of this genre. His comedy is no longer rollicking and boisterous, but more melancholy and probing—suggesting "the pensive light of closing day."

Sometime between 1610 and 1612 Shakespeare returned to Stratford to live the life of a country gentleman, and to take charge of family concerns. Only occasionally did he return to London for brief visits. His contributions to the drama were negligible after 1612. He collaborated with Fletcher in *Henry VIII*, but his contribution to *The Two Noble Kinsmen* and *Sir Thomas Moore* was so slight the plays are not included in the "canon," or list of his plays. His contribution to the theater of his day virtually at an end, Shakespeare died at his home in Stratford a couple of months after making out his will.

*T*here are thirty-seven plays in Shakespeare's canon, and thirty-six of them were published in 1623, seven years after his death. Only *Pericles* is missing. No one knows why. Some scholars believe that Shakespeare's contribution to the play (over his sources, Twine and Gower) lies in the shipwreck scene. But the play is lacking in motivation and unity of action that Shakespeare knew so well how to provide, and had demonstrated many times before.

One of the remarkable things about Shakespeare's survival as a dramatist is that the theater can take little credit for it, and several reasons for that have been given. The first edition of his plays, the famous First Folio edition, did not appear until 1623, seven years after Shakespeare's death. It was assembled by two former members of Shakespeare's company, John Heminge and Henry Condell, who obtained the texts from sources available to them at the time, including quarto editions and theater "prompt-books." In spite of all the errors and omissions, the First Folio was a remarkable achievement. Of the thirty-six plays published, eighteen had been published earlier in quarto editions, that is, as separate plays. Six of them were "bad quartos," shortened versions of the plays that were published without permission and based, often, on no more than actors' memories.

Subsequent editions came out in 1632, 1663, 1664, and 1685; but there was careless editing in all of these, with many omissions, misprints, and faulty punctuation. After the execution of King Charles I by the Puritans in 1642, the theaters were closed because of their "indecency," and they remained closed until 1660, when Charles II was brought back from France and crowned King of England.

With the "restoration" of the English monarchy, the theaters were reopened and went through a period of great change and experimentation. But the theater was now in the hands of "literary" people, and they were the ones who determined what the drama ought to look like. But, more than that they decided what characteristics would reflect Shakespeare as a dramatist. What they all agreed upon was that Shakespeare needed to be improved. Ben Jonson's reputation was greater than Shakespeare's in the second half of the seventeenth century, when Shakespeare was considered a talented writer who lacked discipline. John Dryden, in an admirable essay in 1668, wrote that he admired Jonson for being "the more correct poet," but he loved

Shakespeare who had no need of books to read nature "but looked inward and found her there." That was but an echoing of Milton's reference to Jonson's "learned sock" and Shakespeare's "native wood-notes wild." The first critic to recognize his genius, Dryden wrote that Shakespeare, "of all modern, and perhaps ancient poets, had the largest and most comprehensive soul."

For the next fifty years most of Shakespeare's plays were not staged at all, and those that were produced underwent substantial alteration. Characters were added or dropped as seemed appropriate, scenes were entirely omitted or heavily altered, with a more modern form of English substituted for Shakespeare's language. As a result the public did not see Shakespeare's *King Lear*, but Nahum Tate's, with its happy ending. Cordelia's marriage to Edgar supplied the missing "poetic justice," and Tate's version of *King Lear* was the only form presented on the English stage until the middle of the nineteenth century. Moreover, the public did not see Shakespeare's *Taming of the Shrew*, but John Lacey's; not Shakespeare's *Macbeth*, but William Davenant's. John Dryden and Davenant rewrote *The Tempest*, adding several characters to it; and, under Thomas Purcell's inspiration, it became a musical. Many times actors were instrumental in popularizing a Shakespeare play by their own interpretation of its meaning.

The eighteenth century produced a few notable Shakespearean actors, such as David Garrick, and Sarah Siddons, but Shakespeare as the Elizabethans knew him was banished from the stage. The staging of authentic Shakespeare plays had become a lost art, and no one seemed to be in a particular hurry to rediscover it. But interest in Shakespeare continued to increase, and publications of his plays during the eighteenth century was accompanied by extensive criticism. Rowe, in his 1714 edition of Shakespeare, was the first to provide a biography. Pope followed his own notion of language and meter for the plays; but it was not until Theobald's 1733 edition, with its three hundred or more emendations, that any real restoration of Shakespeare began. Samuel Johnson continued to lament the lack of poetic justice in Shakespeare's plays, complaining that they seemed to have no moral purpose, and that Shakespeare sacrificed "virtue to convenience." He considered many of Shakespeare's comic sexual passages vulgar, but he praised Shakespeare for holding up a "faithful mirror of manners and of life." After Johnson, Shakespearean scholarship was chiefly advanced by the great German critics, Lessing, Goethe, and Schlegel.

It has been argued that while the dramatists of

the seventeenth and eighteenth centuries showed a total disregard for Shakespeare's genius, their intentions were at least honorable. But even that could not be said of some of the nineteenth century dramatists, whose interests in him were more financial than artistic. Atrocities in staging Shakespeare, such as presenting *Henry V* in five scenes, four of which did not appear in the original, were commonplace in the nineteenth century.

It was these abbreviated but colorful versions of Shakespeare's plays that were to find their way to the ends of the English-speaking world—to small settlements and mining camps not only in Canada and the United States, but also in Australia and New Zealand. Not that there was anything strange about exporting Shakespeare in that manner. In his time plays taken into provinces during the off-season months—generally in summer—were often abbreviated versions of longer plays.

During the Romantic Age Shakespeare was respected and promoted by men like Coleridge, Lamb, and Hazlitt, but he was not promoted as a dramatist. His plays were studied as non-dramatic literature. Some early nineteenth century authors regarded his plays as unsuitable for the stage. The drama of this period is sometimes referred to as "closet drama," a poem in dialogue, and printed to be read, rather than acted. It was ostensibly an effort to continue the tradition of Shakespeare and others after the stage had forsaken it. Closet drama, however, was not an invention of the nineteenth century. John Milton's *Samson Agonistes* (1671) is an early example.

In the latter part of the nineteenth century, a concentrated effort was made to restore Shakespeare's plays to their original form as dramatic productions, with publishers attaching themselves to the cause. A more careful editing of his work began, accompanied by a more scholarly interest in Shakespeare's remarkable dramatic gifts. The *Third Variorum*, in twenty-one volumes, appeared in 1821; and the Cambridge edition, in nine volumes, was published from 1863-1866, and served as the basis for many later popular editions.

But what was needed in order to have a new Shakespeare was a new audience and a new theater, and that was accomplished by education. The publisher had succeeded in creating a reading public assisted by college literature classes specializing in Shakespeare. By the twentieth century Shakespeare's reputation was reaching its peak. In the early decades of this century, however, Shakespeare was still not

largely the centerpiece of theater departments, if he was produced at all by them. Representative Shakespearean plays were, however, a part of every anthology of English literature published in the forties and fifties; and they were studied by English literature students in almost every college and university in the English-speaking world.

Shakespeare became the darling of the dramatic stage with the establishment of the repertory theater, committed to the preservation of his plays. The National Theater which took over the Old Vic in 1963, and the Royal Shakespeare Company, with its theater in Shakespeare's hometown, are the most visible in England. The Stratford Shakespearean Festival in Ontario presents Shakespeare each year in Canada. In America notable Shakespearean festivals can be found in almost every state, from New York City to San Diego, California. Occasionally, a notably successful Shakespearean festival appears where one would not, perhaps, expect to find it, as in Cedar City, Utah.

And, during the past quarter century under the aegis of "World Shakespeare Congress", critics, scholars, directors, and actors have been meeting once every five years at places like Berlin, Tokyo, and Los Angeles.

In the last half of this century, three hundred years after his success as a dramatist had been established, Shakespeare's influence remains pervasive, so much so says British director Peter Brooks that "we are faced with the infuriating fact that Shakespeare is still our model."

To review Shakespeare's career in the theater and his subsequent influence does not fully convey the force of his genius. He invented no form of the drama, and he founded no school of followers, as Jonson had done; but it is generally conceded that he achieved supremacy in all its fields. Marlowe may have excelled in one area of the theater, Lyly in another, and Kyd in still another, but Shakespeare was supreme in all aspects of the theater. It has been said of him, "His versatility is as far beyond praise as it is beyond blame. Notice the range of his plays, his mastery of blank verse, the strength and beauty of his poetry, his command of words, his range of experience, and his unequalled powers of creating character. So much a part of the world's speech and thinking has Shakespeare become that we can no more measure his influence than we can measure the influence of the Bible."

Jonson was right: He "was not of an age, but for all time."

CURIE

BY
JERRY
ANDERSON

# Marie Curie
## 1867-1934

> " *C reatures who feel as keenly as I do, and are unable to change this characteristic of their nature, have to dissimulate it at least as much as possible.*"

*E* ve Curie's biography of her mother presents Marie as a woman in the body of a scientist. Robert Reid's biography presents Madame Curie as a scientist in the body of a woman. The works complement one another, each introducing material the other deems unworthy of recording. To arrive at a balanced view of Marie Curie, both books should be read. Both are well written. They, along with a large number of briefer treatments are used extensively in this account of Madame Curie.

Maria Salomee Sklodowska was born on November 7, 1867, of poor but intellectually respected parents, who found it necessary to teach in order to support their family. In fact the intellectuals were highly regarded by Poles during the latter part of the eighteenth century and early years of the nineteenth, because it was they who provided the glue for a country divided as a result of the occupation of Poland by Russia.

Marie (she changed her name from Maria when she enrolled in the Sorbonne in Paris) revealed herself to be exceptionally precocious as a child. Although a couple of years younger than most of the other children in her class, she found school easy. She was especially fond of math, history, literature, German and French. But she read all kinds of material that she had access to, including adventure stories.

The gymnasium she attended in Warsaw was run by the Polish government, but it boasted excellent teachers. When she graduated at age 16, she received a gold medal for being first in her class. After her graduation from the gymnasium, Marie attached herself to the Floating Universities—attic rooms, mostly, where students in Russia-dominated Poland could look for intellectual sustenance. Teaching in them, and even attending them, involved some risk. Being caught could result in banishment to Siberia. But the attraction was too great for Marie to pass up. She loved the informality of it all, and the chance to continue her studies in a variety of subjects.

When she was only eighteen, Marie took a job as a governess, in a well-off family in the country, tutoring the two youngest children. The eldest son began a serious relationship with Marie, and marriage was even discussed. Intimacy at any stage was difficult for Marie to achieve because of her experience with her own mother, who never embraced, touched, or gave physical comfort to her children. The cold indifference of a mother whom Marie genuinely loved left a permanent mark on her, and the young man's sudden breaking off of the relationship was a severe blow to Marie's sense of self.

About this time her older sister, Bronia, who like Marie had received a gold medal at the gymnasium, announced her intention to study medicine in Paris. Women, then, were denied access to higher education in Poland; so, to pursue it, they had to leave the country. Such a decision naturally resulted in physical, financial, and emotional hardship. In Bronia's case, it meant that Marie and her father would have to save money from their meager earnings to assist with Bronia's expenses. It also meant that Bronia, would, after securing employment as a doctor, assist Marie with the expenses of her higher education.

Paris was the city of choice because of the excellent reputation achieved by the Sorbonne, one of the best schools in Europe at the time. And, in France, where freedom was especially valued, no feelings or beliefs were rejected, even if expressed by a woman. At the Sorbonne, teachers were offering biology, mathematics, sociology, chemistry, and physics. Sociology was a new subject, with the name given to it by Auguste Comte, whose works on *Positive Philosophy* had appeared between 1830 and 1854. Marie was not attracted to the social theory of Marx, simply because it promoted internationalism; more to her liking were the theories of Auguste Comte, whose philosophy of Positivism offered a solution to social problems based on science.

But Marie had now shifted her interest from mathematics and physics to physics and chemistry as subjects for specialization. Eight years had passed since her graduation from high school (the academy). She was now twenty-four years old, and the time had come to call on Bronia to fill her part of the agreement. Her sister had graduated from the Sorbonne with her degree in medicine and had married a fellow student, also a doctor. Marie was able to raise enough money to make the trip by rail to Paris. She traveled third class in a railway car that was almost as bare as a freight car.

She arrived in Paris just before the opening of the Fall session, moving in with Bronia and her brother-in-law; and on November 3, 1891, she signed up, under the name Marie Sklodowska, as a student of the Faculty of Sciences at the Sorbonne, a university which her father had called an "abridgement of the universe."

She had few physical needs and lived a spartan and solitary existence. But she was happy. "All my mind was centered on my studies," she wrote. "All that I saw and learned that was new delighted me. It was like a new world opened to me, the world of science, which I was at last permitted to know in all liberty."

Physically, her first years at the Sorbonne were difficult ones. She had to climb six flights of stairs to her attic room every day. The room was furnished with a folding iron bed, a stove, a wooden table, a kitchen chair, a wash basin, a kerosene lamp, a pitcher for water which was drawn from a tap on the landing, and a small heater on which she cooked her meals.

She had two large sacks of coal for the entire winter, which she carried up six flights of stairs, bucketful by bucketful. Sometimes, to save fuel, she neglected to light the stove. The light of her room was so inadequate that she often worked in the gas-lit library at school, where the door stayed open until 10:00 p.m.

Her devotion to her studies permitted no time for friendship or for love. She charted her progress from course to course in her notebooks, from physics and calculus in 1891, to electricity and mechanics in 1892, to electrostatics and kinematics in 1893. In 1893 she placed first in the master's examination in physics. A year later she placed second in the master's examination in mathematics.

Nothing could compete with the satisfaction she got from her commitment to pure science. Working in the light of the lamp in her attic room, Marie felt a bond with the great scientists of the past who detached themselves from place and time in order to pass beyond the limits of accumulated knowledge. But this meant a dedication to pure, not to applied science. On this view science was carried out only so that knowledge could be expanded and transmitted. Application of knowledge, even for the solution of practical problems, had no relevance for the scientist's orientation.

*M*arie met Pierre Curie for the first time while visiting the home of a Polish physicist and his wife. Pierre had been a brilliant student, earning a bachelor of science at sixteen and a master in physics at eighteen. At nineteen years of age, he was a laboratory assistant at the Sorbonne, had made many important scientific discoveries himself, and had patents on several of them. Eventually he became head of the laboratory at the school of physics and chemistry of the city of Paris, where he discovered such things as the Curie law of magnetism and the ultra-sensitive Curie scale.

Because of their mutual interest in science, Marie and Pierre developed an instant admiration for one another, but her natural reclusiveness and her acquired frigidity made winning her over an uphill battle. He often chided her about her Slavic and sometimes childish ideas concerning life and duty. In time he altered her behavior sufficiently for her to alter her attitudes; and on July 26, 1895, they were married. Their first daughter, Irene, was born two years later in 1897.

By the end of 1897 Marie had to choose a subject for her doctorate thesis. A natural choice would appear to be x-rays. Sifting through reports about recent studies in science, Marie was attracted by a discovery made by Henri Becquerel. He had found that uranium salts emitted rays of some unknown nature, even without exposure to light; and these rays, like x-rays, penetrated matter. Becquerel had already published nine papers on it, but he was losing interest in the subject. The cause of the rays was as yet unknown, and Marie would be the one to name the phenomenon.

There were no buildings at the Sorbonne which could be spared for Marie's experiments on the pitchblend ore which contained the Becquerel rays. A shed once used by the school of medicine for its dissection of cadavers, now abandoned and poorly furnished, was all that the Curies could find. It was damp and cold, but in that shed the Curies worked for almost four years from 1898 to 1902, attempting to unlock the mysteries of radioactivity.

Marie's work on uranium rays was carried out using the methods of science and the apparatus invented by Pierre. She surmised that uranium might be only one of several elements capable of emitting radiation. One of her first discoveries was that radiation was some kind of atomic property. She experimented first with all known chemical bondings, in both a pure state and in compounds. She discovered that the compound of thorium emitted rays with an intensity similar to that of uranium. It became clear to her that the minerals contained a radioactive substance much more powerful than either uranium or thorium. Since she had already examined all known chemical elements, she could conclude only that the mysterious substance was a new element. But it became necessary to assign a distinct name to what Marie was con-

vinced was a property of atoms. She gave it the name "radioactivity," and chemical substances containing this "radiance" were called "radio elements."

By now Pierre was so caught up in Marie's work that he abandoned his research on crystals to assist her efforts. Thus began a collaboration which would last for eight years. Working with pitchblende they separated all the elements and measured the radioactivity of each. By this process of elimination, they got two new elements, polonium—which Marie named after her native country—and radium. The radioactivity of radium, they concluded, must be enormous; but it existed in so few traces as to elude isolation.

The physicist colleagues of the Curies had difficulty accepting the new discovery, because it upset the fundamental theories on which science had been based for centuries. The spontaneous radiation of radioactive bodies could not be accounted for. The chemists were even more skeptical. A chemist can accept a new substance only when it submits itself to examination—the chemist must see it, weigh it, touch it, test it with acids. The problem the Curies faced was that no one had seen radium, no one had determined its atomic weight. No one had assigned it a number in the table of elements. And to accomplish all this, Marie and Pierre had to labor for years. By 1898 Marie was publishing articles on her research, and in 1902, forty-five months after announcing the probable existence of radium, Marie was finally successful in preparing a decigram of pure radium from the tons of uranium ore she had examined. She determined its atomic weight to be 225.93 and established it as the 88th known element. The chemists could no longer deny its existence.

In its purified state—as a chloride—radium appeared to be a white powder, much like table salt; and its properties, now becoming better known, were astonishing. Its radiation, for example, was two million times stronger than that of uranium, so that only a thick plate of lead could stop its rays. But there were other strange phenomena connected with radium. It produced its own ghost, or shadow, a gaseous substance—its "emanation"—which was not only active but self-destructive. And it gave off heat. In one hour it produced enough to melt its own weight of ice, enough to increase its temperature as much as ten degrees centigrade above surrounding air. Radium also gave off light, enough to read by, according to Marie. And this light-giving power produced phosphorescence in many substances such as diamonds, which cannot by themselves produce light. Moreover, radium was "contagious." Everything it touched or came near soon took on its "emanation." But it would be a long time before Marie would become aware of the danger of handling radium, and very few precautions were taken while carrying on experiments in the laboratory.

*T*he Curies were, however, alert to the therapeutic effects of radium. They became convinced that it could be used to treat certain forms of cancer. Pure science was forced to yield to the staggering implications of the practical uses to which radium could be put, and a whole new industry came into being, practically over night. Marie never considered the option of patenting the results of her work. It would, she said, be contrary to the scientific spirit. She would accept no monetary gain from her remarkable discovery. Besides, it was the duty of scientists to publish immediately the results of their researches so that the sum of human knowledge can be added to. That commercial ventures could be spun off scientific discoveries was accidental—it was not what science was about. Of one thing Marie was sure—science is not about profit.

The Nobel Prize in Physics for 1903 was rewarded half to Henri Becquerel and half to Pierre and Marie for their discoveries in radioactivity. It was only the third year the Nobel Prizes had been offered. From that moment on, their lives were never the same. It did mean, however, that the Curies could

devote themselves full time to their lab and even take on an assistant. In time many assistants would be employed, each one carefully interviewed by Marie to determine the applicant's qualifications.

But fame came at a heavy price. The Curies, for whom research in radioactivity was still in its infancy, lost the things they valued most—intimacy, silence, and meditation. They were besieged by requests for information from all over the world. The unceasing intrusion by the outside world only added to Marie's antisocial nature. But her mothering instinct was heightened by the birth of their second daughter, Eve, in 1904. Seven years separated the two girls.

Now a chair of physics was created for Pierre at the Sorbonne. Marie joined him as his chief assistant at the lab, and soon afterwards she received her doctor's degree with very high honors. To outsiders, Marie and Pierre appeared to have all that made life valuable, but the strain of their work greatly diminished their health, which their close friends easily noticed.

Marie's life fell apart on April 19, 1906. Pierre was killed that afternoon while crossing a busy Paris street. His head was crushed by the rear wheel of a heavy horse-drawn cart after he slipped and fell on the wet cobblestone street. Marie never fully recovered from the tragic loss of her husband. The French government offered a national pension in the Curie name, but Marie turned it down. She could, she said, take care of herself and her two daughters by her work. She did, however, accept Pierre's chair in physics at the Sorbonne.

In receiving Pierre's chair, Marie became the first woman faculty member in French higher education. The award had been made by the faculty of science at the Sorbonne. On the day of her inaugural lecture, she resumed Pierre's course at the point where Pierre had left it, reviewing the progress of the understanding of the structure of matter since the beginning of the nineteenth century.

A few months after Pierre's death, Marie's work was questioned by the dean of British scientists, Lord Kelvin, who, though he was kind to Marie in person, was not above challenging her conclusion that radium was an element. Ignoring the scientific journals available to him, Kelvin revealed his skepticism in the columns of the London *Times*. It had been discovered by a couple of British scientists that radium spontaneously gives off the enert gas helium, helping to explain the disintegration process of radioactive substances. Kelvin pointed out that lead is one of the disintegration products of radium, and that radium was, rather than a new element, a molecular compound of lead and five helium atoms.

Marie Curie was naturally chagrined by the firestorm that followed Kelvin's theory. Her whole career was at stake, not to mention the basis of the discovery for which she was awarded a Nobel Prize—that radioactivity is an atomic property of the element radium. She went to work in her meticulous way to corroborate her theory. In 1907 she produced four decigrams of what she considered "perfectly pure radium chloride," which enabled her to determine a more precise atomic weight.

Next, she tackled the question of whether polonium, her first discovery, was a metal. The problem for Marie was that there was five thousand times less plutonium in pitchblende ore than there was radium. A ton of the ore contained only a few thousandths of a gram of polonium. After much exacting work, she was able to obtain a sample of polonium salt which was fifty times more radioactive than the same amount of radium salt.

But it was not until 1910, four years after Kelvin's newspaper broadside, that she was able to distill enough radium salt to a shiny white solid, proving what she had said radium was, a metal, and an element. She had even determined its boiling point to be about seven hundred degrees centigrade.

By now Marie was an acknowledged leader of the scientific world. Her influence was enormous and her collaboration with her husband largely forgotten. Setting the International Standard for radium suddenly became of paramount importance, because hospitals were using radium in the treatment of cancer, and knowing what dosage to use meant knowing what a dose was. She insisted that she be the one to establish the standard.

Her *Treatise on Radioactivity*, which ran to nearly a thousand pages, was a summary of the work done in radioactivity. Some of the researchers on the subject believed that while she spent much time crediting the work of other scientists in other countries, she set too much importance on the priority of the work of French scientists, if not on the work of herself and Pierre.

Since her husband's death, Marie had, through her own efforts, become the most widely recognized scientist in France. Her

work was meticulous and focused, and her fellow scientists eagerly looked forward to her publications. But it would be a mistake to view Marie Curie's life simply as that of a woman reaching the pinnacle of success in a man's world as a result of her brilliant mind and hard work. Though they are not treated in summaries of her life and work, nor even in more extended accounts, there existed those occasions that stretched her to her physical and mental limits. The year 1910, for example, was not a particularly good year for Marie. While only in her early forties, she suffered from a variety of illnesses. She was considered by some to be a hypochondriac, chiefly because of her inclination to use her poor health as an excuse for missing social appointments, even at professional conferences. Her attacks of nervous exhaustion, it was said, came "when it suited her." But all this had not prevented her from becoming one of the most respected women in Europe. Even so, when she was offered the Legion of Honor that year, she refused to accept it.

But if 1910 was a bad year, 1911 was worse. It was, by all accounts, the worst year of her life. Marie herself had published numerous articles and several books, but when she applied for an opening in the Academy of Sciences—to which a woman had never been elected—she failed to gain admittance by a single vote. Her interest in gaining membership seemed strange to some, owing to her bitterness over the rejection that Pierre experienced upon his application for membership in the Academy, and her disgust with the whole electoral process. But she reasoned that membership would be good for her laboratory and the work she was trying to accomplish there.

But far more serious problems lay ahead for her. She was accused by the press of having an affair with a married man, the father of four children. The man, Paul Langevin, was a famous and respected scientist and a former pupil of Pierre Curie. Langevin had a reputation for being a top-rate physicist who had made important contributions to the understanding of magnetism. He had arrived independently at the same conclusions regarding the relationship between mass and energy as Einstein, and by 1914 he was aware of the implications of the special theory of relativity.

Langevin's marriage, however, was in a shambles, and it was affecting his work. He often confided to a mutual friend of his and Marie's that he could not go on. Marie and her friend, the daughter of the dean of the faculty of science at the Sorbonne, seemed to feel that Paul was too important to be lost to science, and both women offered him encouragement and comfort.

But of all the notable women in Europe during the early years of the twentieth century, Marie Curie seemed the least likely candidate for such a charge leveled against her. From all that is known of her, she had not the inclination, the health, nor the time for such conduct. The evidence for the charge was reported with all the tastelessness and salaciousness that the French press, which had recently discovered the meaning of "yellow journalism," could supply, with references to Langevin as "a cad and a scoundrel," and Marie as "the vestal virgin of radium." Letters between them had been discovered and printed in a Paris newspaper, and soon reports of the alleged affair were being telegraphed to major cities around the world.

It has been pointed out that there was nothing in the so-called affair that could be said to be unquestioningly incriminating, even in the letters of Marie to Paul. It was suggested at the time that the contents of the letters had been misrepresented, that awkward terms used in them by Marie were due to the Polish meaning assigned to French words, and that other problems of a like nature were involved. But, innocent or not, Marie was devastated by the attacks in the press and by outraged citizens who gathered outside her house. She had to be removed from her home and watched over until the interest in what her daughter referred to in her diary as "the Langevin affair" subsided. In the meantime, she considered suicide. She was the subject of four duels fought in behalf of her honor (several others failed to materialize), and she discovered that her brother and two sisters had taken a train from Warsaw to rescue her.

Notification came in November of 1911 that she was to receive a second Nobel Prize, this time in chemistry. It has been suggested that the second award was made to salve her wounds, that she was awarded the prize twice for essentially the same work, even though the word "radium" was not used in the description of the first award. Marie, however, entertained no such doubts and made clear in her acceptance speech that her work, and hers alone, justified such an honor.

The trip to Stockholm to receive the award took the last bit of physical and mental reserve she could summon up, and she returned to Paris depressed and exhausted. In December she was carried on a stretcher to a nursing home, and it was not until the summer of 1912 that she got the convalescence she required at the home of a friend in England.

In 1913 Marie opened up a radiological laboratory in Warsaw and actually directed it from Paris. Her own laboratory was opened near the Sorbonne and the Pasteur Institute on the Rue Pierre Curie on July 1, 1914. It was called the "Institute de Radium, Pavilion Curie." She prepared with her own hands a gram of radium, her own private property worth at that time in excess of one million gold francs, and made a gift of it to the laboratory.

After a serious kidney operation, she took time for an extended walking tour. She was accompanied by Albert Einstein and his son. Their relationship was referred to as "the comradeship of genius."

When World War I broke out, Madame Curie made an even greater gift of her time and energy. Her contribution to the war effort was extraordinary. She outfitted a Renault automobile with a roentgen apparatus and a dynamo for power. That made it possible to operate the x ray machine by the automobile's motor. To get her car to the front lines safely, she had a red cross painted on it and a French flag attached. She even trained herself as a mechanic so that she could personally service the car. She was able to clean the carburetor and change the tires. Over time she outfitted twenty radiological cars. The army called them "Little Curies." In the course of the war, over one million men were examined in these facilities.

In May of 1921, Irene and Eve, Marie's daughers, were invited along with their mother to the United States—the first of two tiring trips to America that she was to make. An American journalist, Marie Meloney, who was to become one of Marie Curie's closest friends, had discovered that the supply of radium was dangerously low in the Curie laboratory. She formed a fund which in 1920-21 raised $100,000 to buy another gram of radium, and she asked Marie Curie to accept a visit to America to meet with the generous women who were instrumental in raising the money, and to accept the gift of radium from President Harding.

At age fifty-four, Marie took on, for the first time in her life, the obligations of an extended journey. In New York a large group of people had been waiting five hours for the ship to arrive, including a delegation of three hundred Polish women, waving red and white roses. Marie was mobbed by people in every city she visited. She recieved medals and doctorates by the dozen during her tour of the United States; they account for a large portion of the hundred and three honorary titles she was to receive during her career, including seventeen honorary doctorates.

On May 20, 1921, at the White House, President Warren G. Harding presented her with the gram of radium for her laboratory. A planned trip to the west coast had to be canceled, owing to the physical drain the tour imposed on her health.

*H*er trip to America did serve to prepare Marie for several other journeys. She traveled in the ensuing years to countries all over the world, visiting Poland, Italy, Holland, Belgium, England, Spain, and even Brazil. The purpose of these travels, which she always found unpleasant, was to raise money to support her laboratory and the work of her students. The League of Nations appointed her a member of the International Committee on Intellectual Cooperation. And an old provincial capital of China placed her portrait in a temple of Confucius.

On December 26, 1922, a large crowd filled the amphitheater of the Sorbonne to see Marie become the first woman appointed to the French Academy of Medicine. By now, Marie was at the pinnacle of her fame, devoting her studies to the chemistry of radioactive substances and their application.

In 1929, once again, through the collective efforts of the generous women of America, enough money was raised to purchase a second gram of radium, this time for the institute in Warsaw, headed up by Marie's sister Bronia. Marie Curie was obliged once more to take a ship to America. Marie was successful in gaining for herself from this second trip both a pension and an annuity. But one thing about the tour had not changed: "Remember, dear friend," she wrote Marie Maloney, "that I must not have in my program, autographs, portraits and handshakes." In spite of the worst economic depression of the twentieth century, Americans once again responded to the fund-raising efforts of Marie's supporters. On Sunday she took a joyride from New York to Long Island. On Wednesday the panic selling on Wall Street began. The next day was black Thursday. Marie Curie's timing in the raising of funds could not have been better.

When she was sixty-five years of age, she often was still working twelve hours a day. Very seldom did she take time off for personal reasons. Irene and Eve often found her on the floor of her study, surrounded by her papers, slide rules, and monographs, working till the late hours of the evening. She was continually plagued with the necessity to visit government agencies, seeking subsidies and scholarships for the laboratory which she continued to direct. Between 1919 and 1934 the physicist, and chemists at her laboratory published 483 scientific papers, thirty-one of them written by Marie herself.

Her health, always delicate, continued to decline. In 1923, 1924, and in 1930 she had four operations on her eyes. Embarrassed by her condition, she attempted to conceal her poor eyesight from her colleagues and students, but they were not deceived. Her death from aplastic pernicious anemia came as a result of her exposure to radium over a period of thirty-five years. She died on July 6, 1934, in a sanatorium to which she had been anonymously admitted. She gave instructions that all papers dealing with her private life be destroyed. All that remained were the love letters Pierre had written to her while she was a young woman.

JEFFERSON

BY
JERRY
ANDERSON

# *Thomas Jefferson*
## 1743-1825

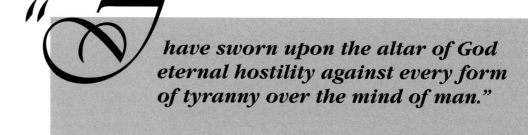

*"I have sworn upon the altar of God eternal hostility against every form of tyranny over the mind of man."*

It would be difficult to imagine a person more consumed by the passion for freedom than Thomas Jefferson, one of the great figures of human history. His name is inextricably linked to America's most cherished ideals, and scarcely a generation has passed since his death in 1826 that hasn't invoked his name and his principles as a panacea for the nation's ills.

The adulation of the man and his principles (the two are practically inseparable) is never more apparent than when the issue of human freedom is raised. Relatively few manifestos have been issued in support of individual human rights, and none more eloquent than Jefferson's Declaration of Independence. Not only did that remarkable document rally the colonists of Jefferson's day, but people in countries of the world where human rights have been callously and systematically disregarded continue to be inspired by the message.

The most cursory view of world affairs makes it painfully apparent that the cause of human freedom has not forcefully and finally been won. The last impressive manifesto in the cause of liberty was adopted by the then fledgling General Assembly of United Nations in San Francisco on December 10, 1948, under the title, "Universal Declaration of Human Rights," but the list of human rights that signatory nations were to recognize has often been flagrantly disregarded, if not largely discredited.

The truths which Jefferson believed self-evident and immutable are obviously neither, and it is appropriate that recognition should be given to those heroes of history who have made some of the most valiant efforts in defense of the freedom of the human mind.

But it is not only Jefferson's authorship of the Declaration of Independence that has inspired admiration for and loyalty to Jeffersonian principles for over two hundred years. Nor is it his accomplishments as a prominent political figure in American politics for forty years, including two terms as President of the United States. What makes Jefferson's approach to freedom so appealing is the breadth and depth of it—his quiet, unrelenting pursuit to expand it to all Americans. His interest extended beyond political freedom to the autonomy of the human mind, not only for Americans, but for people everywhere.

The tree of liberty had not taken root in 1776, when Jefferson gave voice to the passions that were to have such a profound effect on his fellow colonists; and twenty years later, in 1796 when Jefferson was in temporary retirement at Monticello, it was still a sapling struggling to survive a harsh environment. Jefferson himself often expressed his fear that the experiment in self-government might fail. But he realized that for the first time in history the time was ripe to match the theory with the practice.

By the year 1796, Jefferson had spent some twenty-eight years in public service, His years from 1789 to 1793 were particularly difficult ones for him. As George Washington's Secretary of State he had to make difficult foreign policy decisions, but he also had irksome encounters with many in the new government whose views ran counter to his own. Particularly troublesome

were his conflicts with Alexander Hamilton. A great deal of American history in the past two hundred years has been interpreted in terms of the differences between Hamilton and Jefferson. Their views regarding politics were miles apart. Broadly speaking, it may be said that Jefferson cared intensely about the freedom of the individual, while Hamilton put his faith in the strength of the central government; that Jefferson believed that his countrymen were good enough and could be made wise enough to be entrusted with the reigns of government, while Hamilton believed that the common man was neither wise nor good. But there were other significant differences that biographers have been quick to emphasize, because they do much to reveal the political prejudices of these two men. Hamilton wanted to concentrate power, Jefferson to diffuse it. Hamilton feared anarchy, Jefferson feared tyranny. Hamilton was cynical, Jefferson was optimistic. Hamilton believed in heredity, Jefferson believed in environment. Hamilton believed human nature to be static, Jefferson believed it was dynamic. Hamilton favored European methods of government, Jefferson believed new methods were needed.

When Jefferson re-entered politics in 1797 as John Adam's Vice President, he was to encounter more unpleasant years; and often, as before, the question of how to achieve and maintain liberty was central to the issues involved. But the position of Vice President, as inglorious then as it is now, did not permit opportunities for Jefferson to directly affect the outcome of issues he cared most about.

After succeeding Adams as President in 1801, Jefferson was to serve two terms in office, decide against running for a third term though immensely popular, and retire finally and firmly to Monticello where he would spend the remaining years of a long and distinguished life.

About that long and distinguished life much has been written and no attempt will be made here to rehearse more than is warranted to convey a sense of the remarkable character of the man whose principles are indelibly inscribed into the hearts and minds of freedom-loving persons everywhere.

One of the most arresting facts about Jefferson was the all encompassing nature of his intellect. Perhaps the most versatile of the founding fathers, he remains unmatched in our own time, when a command of knowledge like Jefferson's is regarded as something reserved for the geniuses of the earth. He was described as "a gentleman of thirty-two who could calculate an eclipse, survey an estate, tie an artery, plan an edifice, try a cause, break a horse, dance a minuet, and play a violin." But this gives only a partial picture of this remarkable man. He was competent in law, government, architecture, mathematics, medicine, agriculture, language and literature, education, music, philosophy, religion, and almost every branch of the natural sciences from astronomy through meteorology to zoology. Certainly no historic American, with the exception of Benjamin Franklin, could claim competency in so many fields of human thought and action. A review of our history turns up no one who can match his attractiveness to so many people with highly different interests.

*M*any of Jefferson's interests and talents have given considerable attention by the many biographers who have been attracted to him. Of particular interest for this discussion are those to which the cause of freedom can be attached. Others are mentioned for the purpose of helping to reveal the character and intellect of this extraordinary man and to divulge the attractiveness of a free and enlightened mind.

It is not known when Jefferson first became committed to the principle of liberty. Such a focus of attention was hardly to be expected from the son of aristocratic, slave-owning parents, and there certainly were no models of democracy among world governments of Jefferson's time to excite his interest.

His own education offered examples of theoretical models, especially his exposure to John Locke and the French Physiocrats who were advocating a philosophy of human rights scarcely heard of before. Even the timing of Jefferson's life coincided with the advent of the Enlightenment. Perhaps it is more than coincidence that two of America's most prominent representatives of the Enlightenment—Benjamin Franklin and Thomas Jefferson—had spent a significant length of time in Paris, absorbing much of the new political and social thought of the day. He visited the home of one of France's enlightened liberals, Jacques Necker, Louis XVI's Minister of Finance, where he met the Neckers' young daughter Germaine. As Madame de Staël, Germaine was to have occasion later in her life to communicate with Jefferson, whom she much admired.

Another influence that one could hardly disregard as affecting the tenor of Jefferson's thinking about freedom and democracy was his own education. As a boy, he experienced the education provided by the grammar schools of his day—often called "English schools," which can best be described as a classical education, an education which was enlarged during his two years at William and Mary college in Williamsburg. In addition to the smattering of general subjects provided, Jefferson learned Greek, Latin, French, Italian, Spanish and Anglo-Saxon. His competency in Greek and Latin is demonstrated by his tribute to his grammar school teacher: "To read Latin and Greek authors in their original is a sublime luxury. I thank on my knees him who directed my early education for having put into my possession this rich source of delight, and I would not exchange for anything which I would then have acquired and have not since acquired."

In retirement he continued to reveal his standing as an extraordinarily learned man. His accomplishments included, in addition to reading Greek and Latin authors in the original (at age 71 he read Plato's *Republic*), a study of the comparison of the ancient and modern pronunciation of Greek, a study of the New Testament to discover what Jesus *really* said, and the first systematic collection of American Indian dialects.

It is no stretch of the imagination to suggest that Jefferson, like so many of his distinguished predecessors, realized that ignorance is a form of slavery and only an enlightened mind can

truly be regarded as a free one. He was convinced, at any rate, that only an enlightened society was capable of self-government and that an ignorant people, however strong, have no chance of maintaining their God-given freedom given the array of tyrannies poised to deny it.

He often asserted the primacy of education in the struggle for freedom. To Lafayette he wrote (November 20, 1813), "I lay it down as one of the impossibilities of nature that ignorance should maintain itself free against cunning, where any government has once been admitted." And to demonstrate his conviction that education leads to democracy he wrote to Thomas Seymour (February 11, 1807), "It would seem impossible that an intelligent people, with the faculty of reading and right of thinking, should continue much longer to slumber under the pupilage of an interested aristocracy of priests and lawyers, persuading them to disband themselves, and to let them think for them."

Jefferson was to acknowledge, however, in the waning years of his life, that more than the accumulation of knowledge is needed if a society is to maintain itself free of the ills to which it is subject.

He strove incessantly to provide for free public education, but with respect to elementary and secondary schools his efforts were unrewarded. For him the crowning achievement was the establishment of the University of Virginia, which opened in 1825, the year before his death. It was the culmination of a lifelong effort to establish in Virginia "A temple of freedom and a fount of enlightenment."

When the congressional library was destroyed by fire in the War of 1812, Jefferson made available to Congress his own collection of books numbering in excess of six thousand volumes. Jefferson never claimed to have founded the Library of Congress, but, in fact, his library—the best private library in America—was the beginning of it.

More generally known is Jefferson's contribution to the value that ought to be placed on the freedom of political states, though often little attention is given to that contribution beyond his authorship of the Declaration of Independence. When the First Continental Congress which he helped call was convened in 1774, Jefferson was unable to attend owing to illness. At the time he was a member of the Virginia House of Burgesses, the lower house of the Virginia Legislature. Patrick Henry did attend the Congress as a delegate and, upon his return, delivered the impassioned speech in behalf of freedom for which he is appropriately remembered. Jefferson admired much about Henry, and sided with him on most issues. And he was to succeed Henry as governor of Virginia. But in 1774 Jefferson had been in public life for only five years, spending most of his time doing the time-consuming, uninspired tasks which so often fell to legislative committees. He had studied law for five years after college and in 1767 was admitted to the bar.

At the time, then, when the American colonies were wrestling with the proper course of action to take against Great Britain, Jefferson was a young attorney who viewed his age from the standpoint of an enlightened liberal. He was convinced that people should be set free and kept free in order to realize their potential in the light of ever-expanding knowledge. What Jefferson did contribute to the First Continental Congress of 1774 was a paper he had written titled "A Summary View of the Rights of British America." The paper was carefully crafted and won Jefferson attention from outside Virginia. Jefferson's basic position was that the emigrant Britons who founded America possessed the same natural rights of self-government as the emigrant Saxons who founded England. Just as England was not subject to Saxony, America was not subject to England. The early settlers of America had submitted themselves to the King of England, but he was abusing his power. Parliament itself had no rights in the matter. At this point in the rift between England and America, Jefferson's aim was reform of abuse, not secession.

Two years later, in 1776, events had carried the colonists to the point of issuing a proclamation of their declaration of independence. Although five prominent men were appointed to the committee to draft the proclamation—including Benjamin Franklin and John Adams—Jefferson was given the assignment of chief author because the power of his pen was by now widely acknowledged.

The Declaration of Independence was Jefferson's first important contribution to political thought. Though Congress made several revisions in Jefferson's draft, it remains one of the most influential documents ever written. Particularly memorable for the passionate tribute to freedom are the best known lines of the proclamation:

"We hold these truths to be self-evident: That all men are created equal; that they are endowed by their creator with certain inalienable rights; that among these are life, liberty, and the pursuit of happiness...."

It was introduced to the world as "The Unanimous declaration of the thirteen United States of America in Congress, July 4, 1776."

What made the proclamation so compelling was the common sense justification it set forth for revolution—both ethical and legal. Jefferson's commitment to the principle of freedom never revealed itself more clearly than when he wrote the Declaration of Independence. But a share of the creative genius of the proclamation must be given to the liberal spirit which had begun to permeate the colonies by way of France and England.

Upon the completion of his duties with the Second Continental Congress, Jefferson returned home in 1776 to serve in the Virginia Legislature. He began earnestly to pursue his agenda for human rights by starting a full reform of the state's laws and institutions. He had, during the years of the Revolution, demonstrated his unique power of political expression which made him the symbol of ideas which gave hope to those who were inarticulate if not illiterate—as well as those who, like Jefferson, were fully informed about the issues.

The most important of his statutes included abolishing all laws of primogeniture and entail in order to recognize the right to land, establishing elementary and secondary schools for the diffusion of knowledge, and guaranteeing a free press for informed opinion.

One of the most far-reaching of his proposals was the "Statute of Virginia for Religious Freedom" which was not enacted until 1786 when he was in France. The statute called for a complete break between church and state. He was absolutely opposed to the forces in institutions which took away the autonomy of the human mind: "I have sworn upon the altar of God eternal hostility against every form of tyranny over the mind of man." His opposition to tyranny was without qualification. He opposed all forms of political, military, and intellectual tyranny, just as he championed self-government. Even though American freedom might occasionally manifest itself in violence, Jefferson thought it preferable to European tyranny. His motto "Rebellion to tyrants is obedience to God" was grounded in his hope that the spirit of freedom would never die. "The tree of liberty must be refreshed from time to time by the blood of patriots and tyrants," he wrote (in a letter to James Madison, January 30, 1787). That, however, was no invitation to bloodshed as has been so commonly believed. Jefferson was more than an idealist. He was a realist and a utilitarian. His remark was made in reference to Shays Rebellion in Massachusetts in 1786 and of the need for the use of state troops in that conflict before the constitutional convention was called.

One important outcome of his retirement from state politics was the leisure it gave him to write and revise his only book, *Notes on Virginia*. The *Notes* are important not only because of the wealth of data Jefferson supplies about his state, but because they are a reflection of a revolutionary mind. There is, however, one jarring entry in the *Notes* that serves to illustrate the failure of a great mind to make just distinctions. He expressed his conviction that the Negro was inferior and that Blacks and Whites couldn't live harmoniously together. It was one of most unfortunate convictions Jefferson ever expressed, but he was hardly immune to error; and though it is not an excuse to admit that anyone born into an age acquires the predispositions of that age, it would be foolish to believe that one could altogether escape those predispositions.

But Jefferson's opposition to slavery as an institution was firm and permanent. He believed that emancipation was inevitable, but he also recognized the dangers of emancipation and denied the authority of congress to intervene in the domestic affairs of individual states. Originally Jefferson planned to stop the introduction of more slaves into the new nation, to give legal sanction to manumission and to ultimately end slavery as a practice. The only thing the Assembly approved was leaving intact a ban on importing more slaves. In the revision to the constitution in 1785, a proposal was made to limit slavery to the descendants of female slaves living in a state. It was thought that this would eventually eliminate slavery, but the rapid development of cotton plantations doomed that plan.

In regard to his views on slavery, Jefferson could be labeled a racist and a compromiser, but it is unwise to view him apart from the age in which he lived. It is true that he was slow to bring about reforms, but he never upheld slavery. He denounced it publicly for the evils associated with it. It was about slavery as an institution that he wrote, "And can the liberties of a nation be thought secure when we have renounced their only firm basis, a conviction in the minds of a people that these liberties are the gift of God? That they are not to be violated but with his wrath? Indeed I tremble for my country when I reflect that God is just."

Jefferson's initial retirement from politics turned out to be brief. For several months from 1782-1784 he served as a member of the Virginia delegation to the continental Congress, and headed the committee that debated the peace treaty. In 1784 he submitted a bill to prevent the extension of slavery.

From 1784-1789 he was sent off to France with John Adams where they, along with Benjamin Franklin who was in France as minister, were to negotiate treaties with European countries. Franklin and Adams returned home and Jefferson stayed on in Paris as a successor of Franklin as minister to France. The French Revolution had not yet burst onto the world scene, but the makings of it were already apparent. Jefferson was not uncritical of France and the French, but he immersed himself in the culture. He influenced Lafayette and other enlightened aristocrats and was influenced by them. His hope was not that the French monarchy would be suddenly overthrown, but that it would change direction, and allow a greater measure of freedom and self-government. This was perhaps a flaw in Jefferson's thinking, but then Jefferson saw only the opening stages of the revolution in France. His most striking democratic utterances were based on the contrast between European absolutism and American freedom and self-government.

When Jefferson returned home in 1789, he found that he had been appointed Washington's Secretary of State. In his absence, congress had drafted the Constitution in Philadelphia in 1787. It was ratified the next year, but Jefferson was critical of its lack of a Bill of Rights and of the failure to limit the term of the President. His opposition to Alexander Hamilton began in earnest, with Jefferson viewing Hamilton's policies as exceeding the authority of the Constitution. Hamilton belonged to a political party which was gaining a large following from those who favored a strong united government. These High Federalists were opposed by the Democratic-Repub-lican party, which Jefferson would soon himself effectively lead until 1797.

The most important thing Jefferson did was to present the struggle as something more than just political bickering, to emphasize his belief that freedom itself was at stake. But the experience as Secretary of State was not a happy one for Jefferson, and he resigned in 1793, once more to return to Monticello. Although content with his life on his plantation, Jefferson was urged by his followers to run for President in 1796. Running against John Adams, Jefferson came in second, and automatically became, according to the rules of that time, Vice President. At least as Secretary of State he had an official office and some solid tasks to perform. Now, however, he watched with dismay as Congress passed such unpalatable statutes as the "Alien and Sedition Acts." The acts were intended specifically to stifle criticism of the government by the Democratic-Republican Party, which Jefferson led. Because the United States was near war with France, the acts were deemed necessary to control dissent. The laws called for the deportation of aliens and punishment of sedition. Jefferson was not immune. His attempts to explain away the French attitude resulted in his being accused of seditious activities. A clause making adherence to the cause of France punishable by death was eventually omitted, but the office of the Vice President was not protected by the bill.

Jefferson and Madison argued in the Kentucky and Virginia Resolutions of 1798-99 that the Alien and Sedition acts were unconstitutional. Approaching the problem from the position of state rights (his most extreme position on the subject), Jefferson argued for freedom of the individual — personal and political freedom, freedom of speech and of publication—but Jefferson undoubtedly realized that freedom of the individual was not guaranteed by the authority of the states. Fortunately for Jefferson the storm quickly passed away.

During his first term, as President (1801-1805) Jefferson attempted to keep the government on an even course. His policies were conciliatory, and he continued to view government as an institution which existed to protect the individual's right to life, liberty and the pursuit of happiness. In the name of expediency, however, he was more willing to subjugate the immediate interests of the individual to his dream of national unity. Even his purchasing of Louisiana, which doubled the size of the United States, was undertaken with liberty in mind. "By enlarging the empire of liberty," he said, "we multiply its auxiliaries, and provide new sources of renovation, should its principles at any time degenerate, in those portions of our country which gave them birth."

Also during this first term, Jefferson was careful to avoid actions that could be called attacks on the freedom of the press. The revolution of 1800 which thrust Jefferson's Democratic-Republican policies into national prominence was a revival of the "Spirit of 1776," and Jefferson so regarded it. He urged his countrymen to return to the faith and vision of 1776 that recognized the unique character of the American people. Their experiments in self-government, he thought, were destined to set an example for the entire world.

After twelve years of Federalist supremacy, America was to be led by a man who symbolized freedom and democracy. At the time of the Alien and Sedition Acts, the Federalists had attacked individual liberty, which Jefferson had thought was firmly established by the revolution of 1776. The "truths" of the Declaration of Independence were, he thought, self evident and immutable. As President he thought of himself as representing all Americans, and he came to identify national independence and individual freedom with his own party. Americans breathed a freer air during his administration than under Washington or Adams, enjoying the most tolerant government and most democratic society on earth. Jefferson truly sought to make people freer and happier. Though criticized bitterly by the religious leaders of his day, he consistently acted in behalf of the "illimitable freedom of the human mind."

In his second term as President (1805-1809), Jefferson attempted to extend his policy of neutrality abroad and on the high seas, but found it necessary to support the highly unpopular Embargo Act of 1807. The act was seen as contravening the Fourth Amendment provision of unreasonable search and seizure. It was certainly inconsistent with the principle of individual liberty. Thus the Embargo Act seemed wholly uncharacteristic of Jefferson. Believing the country to be in wartime conditions, Jefferson thought it was necessary to restrict enterprise; but he placed no corresponding restrictions on public opinion which he regarded as more important.

As a champion of both freedom and self-government, Jefferson took little interest in promoting the virtue of institutions. As a result he has been charged with contributing little to the office of the presidency.

Upon his retirement from public office in 1809, Jefferson made the final journey to Monticello. In retirement his achievements were as remarkable as they were in public service.

His chief accomplishment was the founding of the University of Virginia, which was chartered in 1819 and opened in 1825, the year before he died. His involvement was complete: He designed the buildings, supervised the construction, selected the faculty, planned the curriculum, and even selected the reading for some courses. Jefferson's influence on American architecture is well known, particularly in regard to the Greek and Roman tradition of public architecture. What is less known is that in 1976, the year of the America Bicentennial, the academic village of the University of Virginia, which Jefferson designed, was voted the proudest achievement of America architecture in the past two hundred years.

Jefferson's accomplishments in science are also remarkable. He mastered the techniques of small pox vaccination, collected fossils, fashioned tools, designed a dry dock, improved agricultural practices, and, of course, sent out, while President, the Louis and Clark expedition. It was characteristic of Jefferson's commitment to science to arrange for Lewis's visit to Philadelphia for training in astronomy, botany, mineralogy, zoology, and Indian history before the expedition was launched.

Jefferson's interest in academic studies has been noted. He believed wholeheartedly in classical education and disbelieved intensely in theological education. He proposed a system of primary, secondary, and tertiary education, to benefit all citizens of a society. The Bill for the More General Diffusion of Knowledge was advanced while Jefferson was still serving in the Virginia legislature in the 1770's. The preamble to the bill laid down two objects. The first was "to illuminate as far as practical, the minds of people at large." The second was to ensure "that those persons whom nature hath endowed with genius and virtue, should be rendered by liberal education worthy to receive, and able to secure the sacred deposit of the rights and liberties of their fellow citizens, and that they should be called to that charge without regard to wealth, birth, or other accidental condition of circumstance."

In 1811 he started his voluminous correspondence with John Adams, whom he had served as Vice-President. About 19,000 letters written by Jefferson survive, the first when he was sixteen years old and was thinking about going to college. His writings have been called "the richest treasure house of historical information ever left by a single man."

But Jefferson is important for more than his educational and humanitarian reforms. The basis of his fame will always be his championing of the rights of man in the spirit of the Declaration of Independence. He will be remembered for his faith in the ability of the American people to govern themselves through representative institutions. A strict constructionist, he believed that the powers of the federal government should be strictly limited in order to protect the rights and well-being of the individual and the state. A life-long advocate of liberty for all and of education for all in proportion to their merit, he revealed himself to be an untiring champion of the common man.

*F*or Jefferson the best form of government would secure the supremacy of the private and free intellect as well as a populistic, agrarian, republican democracy. His championship of state-rights and individual liberties was unfailing. Rarely if ever did he lose sight of his clear-purposed goal of human freedom and happiness. He considered them inseparable. To him freedom of the mind was an absolute. The faith he had in individuals he pronounced and maintained more persistently than almost any of his countrymen. It was this faith in human beings and in the human mind which constitutes his most enduring legacy.

Intellectually he exemplified more conspicuously than any of his fellows the liberal and humane spirit, the incessant quest for knowledge, and the fundamental belief in the power of the human intelligence.

The thread of consistency which runs through his entire career and unites him with lovers of liberty in all generations was not his attitude toward a specific economic system. It was his abiding, passionate faith in the right of men to rule themselves and his undying hostility to any form of tyranny. As a major apostle of individual freedom and human dignity he has belonged not only to his own time but to the human race. When tyranny threatens, men's minds are turned back to this foe of every kind of tyranny. To all who cherish freedom and abhor tyranny in whatever form it manifests itself, he remains an abiding symbol of hope.

On the fiftieth anniversary of the signing of the Declaration of Independence, July 4, 1826, he was too ill to attend the ceremonies in Washington, but sent his best wishes. He died just before 1:00 p.m. His friend John Adams, who died just a few hours later, uttered, as his last words, "Jefferson still lives." It was as much a prophecy as a tribute.

# Madame de Staël
## 1766-1817

*"Jefferson thinks as La Fayette; La Fayette as Wilberforce:...It is in the soul, not in the calculations of self-interest, that the principles of liberty are founded."*

Germaine de Staël was one of the most remarkable women of letters in her time or any time. Her writings include novels, plays, poetry, history, literary criticism, moral and political treatises, and autobiographical memoirs. She had a precocious appetite for ideas on several subjects and an intellectual intensity that made her truly unique. She was recognized for her clear vision of wider issues in the social and political spheres, and of the achievements of civilization and its cultures. Though she was the product of intellectualism and rationalism, she embodied the principles which later would be identified as "romantic," thus helping to affect the transition from Neoclassicism to Romanticism. At the time of her death she was the most important woman in Europe.

Yet, why, it may be asked, is the name Madame de Staël not more widely recognized?

Historically the roles of woman have been different from those of men. Women have more frequently been supporting players than recognized leaders in most fields of human endeavor, even when they possessed exceptional intellectual qualities. It should not be surprising, therefore, that a woman chosen to join the ranks of intellectual giants selected for the Centurium would be a less recognized figure. Although the major pieces of Madame de Staël's own literary works are important and substantial, perhaps the most significant role she played was that of a facilitator of intellectual thought and discussion. This view of her is supported by the conviction that in politics and literature she never pursued extremes, but continued to see herself as a mediator, as a channel of communication. "The calculation of ideas," she wrote, "is of all kinds of commerce, the one whose benefits are more certain." It was aptly said of her, "She makes use of a peculiar talent in being mid-wife to the birth of others' ideas."

But, while it is true that her literary fame is exceeded by her importance in the history of ideas, those ideas are, after all, embodied and admirably expressed in her literature. Interest in that literature has been gathering momentum in recent years, in part because new ways have been found to assess the significance of her contributions.

This attempt to recreate her is founded in the belief that she is not just a curious monument, but a person whose problems and ideas are both relevant and alive in our own age. If Staël and her works are relatively unknown to a generation which is about to slip unobtrusively into the twenty-first century, it is because the issues she cared so much about have long ceased to occupy center stage; but a perceptible change is occurring. In 1803 Staël herself wrote, "A book is its own defense; we are often unfair to people; in the long run we are never unfair to works themselves."

To understand Madame de Staël it is necessary to understand the times in which she lived. Her greatness lies in the fact that her voice was heard above the roar. For three decades—from the eve of the French Revolution until the Bourbon Restoration—she held the spotlight as a political figure, a woman of letters, a philosopher, and a passionate, uninhibited, tragic heroine. Passion and intellect, drama, and, often, comedy are intertwined in Staël's life as well as in the lives of those close to her. She lived a life of noisy exaggeration, but the brilliance of her mind and the intensity of her emotions reveal a fascinating woman. Her time was one of historical transition, and she was a woman to ride the whirlwind. Her courage and determination, her petulance and her vanity were intensely feminine; and, in a world of revolutions, she launched an idealistic rebellion of her own against all that was cynical, tyrannical, and mediocre in French thought and culture of the eighteenth century.

After the defeat of Napoleon at Waterloo in 1814, it was thought appropriately witty to remark that there were three great powers left: England, Russia, and Madame de Staël. If time has not been kind to her, if Germaine de Staël has become a faded name, the reasons are not difficult to find. The problem for Staël was not that she was considered by many to be

mannish, to be virile, to be tasteless, to lack manners, to follow a moral code allowed only to men. Many of her friends and acquaintances offer evidence to reveal that she could display just the opposite quality. She would be courteous, tasteful, gentle, and highly motivated morally. Her crime was not so much that she embarked on so many love affairs, but that she did it openly—not brazenly, just openly. She seduced men not so much by her physical charms, but by appealing to their minds and sensibilities. Her inability to separate her intellectual from her sexual involvements was not so much a failure of morality (and she had a great deal to say about morality in her writings) as the result of the unprecedented momentum of her enthusiasm. She was charged with more than having an "unwomanly" interest in politics and a disregard for the sexual conventions of her time. Her unforgiven sins were her defiance of public opinion, her ruthless pursuit of happiness, her conscious superiority, and her rejection of male supremacy. She appeared, in other words, to lack the requisite portion of female humility. But it is precisely these "sins" that made her

the extraordinary person she became.

As a writer, she aspired to be "literary," to offer judgments about history, about culture, about society, about books. That was the problem. If she had been content to write novels as Fanny Burney or Jane Austen did, so many voices would not have been raised against her; on the other hand, Germaine de Staël would then scarcely have merited a footnote in history. What she did merit was much more! And why she was considered a power in Europe at the time of her death is worth discovering.

*I*t was not merely her political power that won her acclaim. She dominated at least four of the worlds of the period: those of love, literature, politics, and conversation, and she didn't attempt to separate them. She talked incessantly, publicly, and with the utmost brilliance. It is in the areas of literature and politics that she was seen as intruding into a man's world, but she never wrote anything except as a woman, and it is a mistake to misread her androgynous nature as essentially masculine.

Women like Staël attempted to free themselves from the disabilities they suffered in an oppressive society, especially where their contributions to literature were concerned. They felt that there must be a revolution which would change ideas concerning the way women were regarded in the eyes of the law as well as in the minds of men. It was quite natural, then, for Staël to believe that a revolution in letters should accompany the political and social revolution. "Nothing in art must be stationary," she wrote, "and art becomes petrified when it ceases to change."

Of revolution, Staël knew a great deal. Her life covered fifty years of the greatest changes in social, political, philosophic, and literary thought of modern times, and she wielded a vital and significant force in those changes.

Her important work on Rousseau not only demonstrated her competence as a writer, but it also established her as the first major female critic. It was an approach to criticism that would break the tyranny of rules inherited from seventeenth century classicism, which stifled creativity. Readers were asked to judge works according to personal response. Unlike Rousseau, Germaine de Staël did not seek the Golden Age in the past but in man's progressive development.

France, under the Old Regime—the political and social system existing before the Revolution of 1789—was famous for its salons, all of which were presided over by women. And at these salons the most intellectually illustrious men of Europe gathered. After her marriage to Jacques Necker, Louis XVI's minister of finance, Suzanne Necker, Germaine's mother, added her own salon. Though a strict Calvinist, she presided over a strange assembly of irreligious and libertine philosophers. Hers became the most popular salon of the day. Some of the most prestigious men and women of Europe were regular "clients," including Edward Gibbon and Voltaire.

This was also the period known as the Enlightenment. Both Franklin and Jefferson, in Paris at the time, came under its spell. Tallyrand, a friend of Germaine de Staël, remarked that those who had never known this period were ignorant of the sweetness of living. In fact, the Enlightenment saw the art of communication reach its highest level.

No wonder then that it was in her mother's salon that the future Madame de Staël came under the influence of the political ideas of the "philosophes"—"a group of diverse, individualistic Frenchmen" who led the intellectual movement.

Suzanne taught Germaine at home, incorporating the pedagogical ideas of Rousseau, but ignoring his advice for the education of women. Germaine learned to think for herself, to follow the light of her own conscience, to be natural and unrestrained in her dealings with people. Under her mother's tutelage, Germaine received a strict religious training, became proficient in English and Latin, and read and analyzed several texts selected by her mother. But, it is reported, until the age of twelve she had no playmates and she never spent one hour of familiar conversation with her mother.

Soon after her arranged marriage in 1786 to Eric Magnus Staël von Holstein, the Swedish ambassador to Paris, Germaine established her own salon which soon became one of the most frequented salons in Paris. At the age of twenty-four she was already celebrated. Her book on Rousseau, written when she was twenty-two, had made her famous. Now, at a time when women held unprecedented sway in Paris, Germaine de Staël shone supreme, her influence exceeding that of all the others. When she was forced to escape from France in 1792, she transferred her influence to the family home at Coppet, near Geneva.

The story of Staël's banishment from Paris,

later from all of France, gives an indelible picture of her courage and tenacity. There are few episodes in the life of Germaine de Staël more remarkable than her relationship with Napoleon. She baffled Napoleon, even intimidated him. Her struggles with the man who was to conquer all Europe with the exception of England, when it seemed that she alone in all France—indeed in all Europe—dared oppose him, was splendidly courageous. Adding to the fascination of their relationship is the fact that Napoleon's brothers Joseph and Lucien were friends of Staël and remained so all her life.

Initially Staël admired Napoleon and thought he might be good for France. But then Napoleon was making promises he would not keep, and he would soon abrogate all power to himself. Staël became aware early in their relationship that Napoleon might be carried away by ambition and crush what little liberty had been won; she was right. Hearing of the daily reunions in Madame de Staël's salon, where she incessantly promoted the cause of freedom, Napoleon sent his brother Joseph to her as a friend to remind her that what the nation required at the moment was peace, not political discussion that kept everything in a state of agitation. Napoleon was ready to grant her almost anything for her silence. "Ask her what it is she really wants," Napoleon told Joseph. "It is not a matter of what I want," Staël replied, "but of what I think." This was the answer Joseph was obliged to give the First Consul. She even attacked Napoleon on the subject of military spirit, asserting that it would subvert freedom.

Napoleon had been swept to his position as the head of the state on the wave of his military prowess. It was to be expected, then, that one of the first attacks Staël made on Napoleon was on the subject of the military spirit being subversive of freedom. She even drew an analogy between military discipline and that of the church, pointing out that the discipline to which the priests were subjected was intended to destroy the freedom of reason. Napoleon was not amused.

Moreover, Staël's book *On Germany* infuriated Napoleon. Speaking to his brothers Joseph and Lucien on January 17, 1802, he said, "Tell her she's not to try blocking the road I choose to take, wherever it leads, for if she does I will break her, I will smash her." Yet he could be almost gentle with her; and later, when Staël learned that two men were to be sent to assassinate Napoleon, she told Joseph that she wanted to go herself to warn Napoleon of the danger.

Saint-Beuve called Staël the "Empress of Mind," Napoleon the "Emperor of Matter." In the fourteen-year duel between them "the Emperor ended up without any matter, while the Empress had broadened and sharpened her mind."

Germaine de Staël never wrote anything without political intent, and her intention during a good part of her literary life was to bait Napoleon. When *Corinne* was published, the minister of police suggested to Staël that a few laudatory remarks about Napoleon in the preface might make all his anger toward her vanish. The hint was wasted on Madame de Staël. She was not going to have it said of her that she stooped to flatter the Emperor in any way. Napoleon hated the book, but still felt drawn to it. He could see Corinne as the reflection of Germaine, which indeed she was. "Oh," Napoleon exclaimed, "I see her, I hear her, I feel her! I want to fly from her, and—I fling the book from me." Napoleon found the whole spirit of the book, with its constant appeal to liberty, to enthusiasm, distasteful, because it was intended, though ostensibly just a novel, as an appeal for the foundation of a different form of government to what Napoleon had established in France.

As an enemy of Napoleon, Staël was one of the most spied upon women in Europe. As a result, a body of written material was to emerge which would reveal not only the details of her life, both public and private, but the inner intellectual and political history of Europe from the beginning of the French Revolution to the first years of the Bourbon Restoration, as well as literature of Germany, Italy, and England.

Staël's exile lasted for twelve years; but, in exiling her, Napoleon compelled her to be free and to travel widely, to grow, to think, and to write in place of taking action, to hear and to be heard by Europe's most creative intellectuals, not only in their own countries—Germany, Italy, Austria, Russia, Sweden, and England—but gathered around her at Coppet. Out of her travels two books emerged which could not have been written otherwise—the treatise *On Germany* and the novel *Corinne, or Italy*. Both were instrumental in helping literature break free of its neoclassical bonds, and in launching the Romantic movement in France.

Staël's reputation as a writer has remained intact, but she lost ground as a novelist. That, however, is changing. New editions of her novels *Delphine* (1802) and *Corinne* (1807) have appeared in recent years with enthusiastic reports about her relevance for an age she could hardly conceive that some day would exist. Early biographers have discounted her importance as a novelist (*Corinne* was called the worst great novel ever written), but at the same time it was acknowledged that she wielded power over people's minds more for her novels than for her works of ideas. The truth is that all her works are works of ideas, and only now is the importance and relevance of some of those ideas being discovered. Scholars are now bringing light to partially hidden dimensions of *Delphine*, which is more than just a retelling of a classical tale of impossible love.

Both *Delphine* and *Corinne* were enormously successful and won Staël instant acclaim. Napoleon exiled her for writing Delphine, but it was the literary event of the season in England, France, and Switzerland. From 1802-1820 it went through fifteen editions. From 1830-1883, ten more editions were published. *Delphine* deals with life in France during the Old Regime, and showed women what they could not do and be. Staël addressed herself, like Rousseau and Stendhal, to the part of the public who see themselves above society's laws. Thus the very essence of Delphine's character is the liberal credo that truth is relative to the self; it is never absolute.

*Corinne* is a very different kind of story. Goethe led the praise of it, calling it new and fresh. It was an immediate success. From 1807 to 1883, a period of 76 years, it went through forty-two French editions and has had several English translations down to the present time. It was one of the most popular books of the nineteenth century. As the first novel to present the heroine as a genius (the likeness to Staël herself was not lost on those who knew the author), the book showed women their possibilities; and women in France, England, and America took Corinne for their model. Its influence on women who read it was deep and enduring; and the list of the women who read it and were influenced by it, both in Europe and in America, reads like a who's who of female novelists. But men, too, came under its spell, from Byron to Henry James.

*Corinne* also did much to create the Romantic myth of Italy and Italians that still influences our thinking of that nation. It was Staël's first attempt to use natural surroundings as a significant background for her novels, and it touched a generation ready for fresh ways of feeling. The book has much to recommend it, and is credited with attracting Byron and other English expatriots to Italy to live and even die there.

It has been said that Staël did not create a feminist movement any more than she created the Romantic movement. But she certainly stood on the threshold of both, and many qualities that help to define feminism and romanticism are found in her writings. But to the extent she was an overt feminist she was certainly a timid one; she was no more radical in that regard than she was in the political sphere. She shared in the caution of the second generation of those promoting a new feminist ideology, which included assigning a different sphere of life to men and women.

Despite the spontaneity, intensity, and extravaganza of her public persona, Staël remained extremely sensitive and timid at heart. She was known to have suffered throughout her life from a terror of abandonment and a feeling of emptiness. That she could live such an extraordinarily animated life at the social and creative levels testifies to her strength of will and of mind.

Among Staël's earliest writings are the *Essay on Fiction* (1795) and *The Influence of the Passion on the Happiness of Individuals and Nations* (1796). Both are considered highly competent works.

Of fiction, says Staël, the chief purpose is to entertain. The moral of the story must be hidden, or embellished with what moves the heart, such as pride, avarice, and vanity. She admired Richardson and Fielding because their novels employ invented situations but follow real life. She condemned the French novel of her time for its "sterility, coldness, and monotony." The cure, she thinks, can be found in the English novel. These ideas had a great influence on later novelists, notably Stendhal and Balzac. She predicted the emergence of the psychological novel, which would soon make its appearance.

The passions assumed central importance for Staël. The happiness of individuals and nations are affected by the power to improve or worsen their condition. It is the powers of men which make necessary the sacrifice of man's liberty to keep order in a nation.

*On Literature Considered in Its Relation with Social Institutions* (1800) was a truly significant book for its time. It contains over six hundred pages of documented facts, and was written in only a few months. It quickly went into a second edition and boasted many admirers in France and other countries.

The book contains a plea for the emancipation of women. It raises a complaint against "the whole social order's taking up arms against a woman who would aspire to the high reputations achieved by men." Since the theme of the book is the perfectability of the human spirit, Staël argues that women should be perfected like men, individuals like nations.

Staël studies civilizations from the days of Homer to those of the French Revolution. With an amazing power of analysis, she penetrates the history of institutions, social mores, and literature. Of France, she says, "We have founded only hatred and the friends of liberty march in the center of the nation, with heads bowed, blushing for the crime of one group calumniated by the prejudices of the other."

*On Germany*, published in 1810, is generally considered the crowning work of her career as a critic of culture. The book is in the

tradition of Voltaire's *Letters Concerning the English Nation*, published eighty-one years earlier and Tocqueville's *On Democracy in America*, published twenty-two years later. Like Voltaire's *Letters*, it registers a protest against the suppression of intellectual freedom in France, and is a successful attempt to revitalize French thought by introducing fresh ideas from other nations. Like Tocqueville's book, it attempts to delineate a culture broadly defined and to point out to an apathetic public the direction taken by a new nation (which, in a sense, Germany was).

When Staël wrote *On Germany*, neither Germany nor Italy were in the forefront of the nations of Europe. The book brought fresh winds of German Romanticism blowing into France. The author was not asking her countrymen to imitate the Germans, but only to look for their own national treasures.

Staël's *Consideration of the Principal Events of the French Revolution* (1818) is not only the first attempt at a general study of its period but is probably the first treatise in political science by a woman. In it she traces the history of the West from Greek and Roman times, declaring that the nations of Greece and Rome disappeared as a result of their unjust institutions, among which was slavery. The only great nation, according to Staël, is England, which, in mankind's present state of knowledge, appears to be the perfection of the social order. The English constitution is the "finest monument of justice and moral greatness existing in Europe." Staël sees French history as a struggle for liberty confined by law.

If a single word were required to explain Madame de Staël's ideological orientation, it would be "freedom." She would call attention to the way Germans of her day combined great freedom of thought with an inclination to obedience in politics. The tendency would not be confined to German idealists; it would be found among intellectuals everywhere, who would attempt to reconcile the claims of unrestricted freedom with the acceptance of various forms of democracy. Staël herself was ambivalent on this. But then she was not only an ideologist but a realist and a pragmatist, who found it necessary to carry out her program for freedom in many different ways.

Neither Staël nor her father were aware of how far the French had to go to achieve liberty; and although the United States was admired for its ability to create a democracy, there was little resemblance between condi-

tions in the two countries leading up to their revolutions. The liberal thinkers and writers in France deliberated about the rights of the governed, but they lacked practical experience. They had no notion of the dangers inherent in the uprooting of the laws and customs of the Old Regime without having a comprehensive system of justice to replace it. Compromise and moderation became increasingly difficult to achieve; and, while Equality was the slogan advanced for France, Liberty was the cry of all reformers from La Fayette to Desmoulins.

Staël was aware of the dangers of radicalism in the political arena. She had witnessed first hand the excesses of the Reign of Terror and other acts of unbridled passion. She risked her life in helping her friends escape from France when their lives were in danger. She even wrote a pamphlet in defense of Marie Antoinette, who had been kind to her.

For Staël freedom was above all the right for the human spirit to progress. If enthusiasm keeps the spirit alive, fanaticism kills it. In Staël's world conciliation was difficult to achieve because of the fanaticism which does not recognize the legitimate rule of government. In a world where enthusiasm was usurped by fanaticism and where reason no longer held sway, Madame de Staël offered a passionate defense of moderation.

In her 1795 pamphlet *Reflections on Internal Peace*, Staël argued that a republican form of government can only be worked out in a state of peace. Excesses practiced in the instance of liberty must above all be avoided.

Staël believed that political liberty should be distinguished from civil liberty, which belonged to all citizens. But civil liberty itself did not permit distinctions. People would benefit alike from equal taxation and from legal forms of arrest and trial. She advocated a bicameral system for the legislature and an executive without absolute veto powers. She clearly saw as early as 1795, that, if France were to return to a limited monarchy, it would be by way of a military government; but it was a process she did not favor.

Staël possessed a strong faith in the progress of man and his institutions. For this reason she considered a constitutional republic as a guarantee—and perhaps the only guarantee—of liberty. The final chapter of her highly regarded work *Consideration of the Principal Events of the French Revolution* is entitled "Love of Liberty." There she draws attention to the opponents of liberty who in every country are the enemies of thought and discussion. The "enemies" are identified as the Aristocrats who are convinced of the necessity of a monarchy, the men disgusted with and disillusioned by the French Revolution, and the Bonapartists and Jacobins who refused to consult their consciences in the matter of politics.

The elite of a society she identifies as those who serve freedom. In every country such people agree on the abolition of the slave trade (as, she said, England had recently done), on the liberty of the press (her book *On Germany* had been seized and destroyed by Napoleon), and on religious tolerance. "Jefferson," she said, "thinks as La Fayette. La Fayette as Wilberforce." The principles of liberty are to be discovered in the soul, the thought, not in calculations of self-interest.

Her belief that the principles of freedom are the same the world over is a result of her cosmopolitanism, the result of her exile. Her voice was raised in the cause of humanity and freedom everywhere—and Napoleon had only himself to blame for that. Her far-spreading influence was to unite in many directions a hitherto unknown love of liberty and national sentiment. She stirred up a united Europe against an aggressive France, while, at the same time, helping to shape French liberal political theory.

She traveled, during her exile, just ahead of Napoleon's armies, from Austria to Russia, always under surveillance. In St. Petersburg she met Czar Alexander and conferred with him about an alliance with Sweden and England which would free Europe from the tyrant in a war of independence. In that effort she was magnificently successful. Her access to men in the highest positions of government seemed wholly unrestricted. If they were not convinced that the course she recommended was the right one, they were impressed by her firm grasp of political principles and by her commitment to the cause of freedom. When Murat succeeded Joseph as King of Naples, she wrote, "I adore you, not because you are a king, not because you are a hero, but because you are a real friend of liberty."

In her novel *Delphine* she tackles the problem of personal liberty by openly advocating a revolutionary and individual approach to freedom. In Delphine's case, the solution is similar to that of Clarissa in Richardson's novel: The heroine must die.

She offers the radically new notion that love requires freedom to work itself out, acknowledging, however, that this freedom, like moral freedom, can be dangerous. In *Delphine* the characters are free to make their own choices. Delphine shared the existential loneliness of Clarissa, whose flight into death is the only liberating course open to her in the end.

It is almost as though women were destined to be perennial victims of a male-dominated society, where being equal with men is a dream that only foolish women succumb to. In her own time, she thought nature had conspired with society to disinherit half the human race. "Youth gives woman power for a moment, but it is lost for the other half of her life as when she grows old. A man receives all that a woman can give, then disengages himself. Love is the story of a woman's life; it is an episode in man's." Staël urges women to remain in the path of virtue or they will suffer by man-made worldly opinion.

Almost the last words she was known to speak were spoken to Chauteaubriand: "I have always been the same, lonely and sad. I have loved God, my father, and liberty." She was visited just before her death by George Tichnor of Boston, who left a moving record of his visit. She apologized to him for not being as brilliant as she used to be, then prophesied of America, "You are the vanguard of the human race. You are the world's future."

Her death had a profound effect on those who came under her influence. "Her enthusiasm had been so great, her vitality so intense," it was reported, that "when she was gone, they felt that their death, too, had begun. Ten even twenty years after her death her intimates still mourned the period in their lives when she had been their center; and, to those who wanted to know what Madame de Staël had been like, they could only answer, half in pride, half in regret, that no one who had not known her, had not heard her, had not felt her power, could possibly form the least idea of what she was like." The light was so extinguished in some who were close to her that their acquaintances scarcely recognized them.

Today, her ideas still ring true as clarion calls to freedom and civil rights. It is her struggle in behalf of the rights of the individual that gives her new life.

MILL

BY
JERRY
ANDERSON

# *John Stuart Mill*
## 1806-1873

" *There is a limit to the legitimate interference of collective opinion with individual independence; and to find that limit, and maintain it against encroachment, is as indispensable to a good condition of human affairs as protection against political despotism.*"

Perhaps the most compelling reason to acquaint oneself with what John Stuart Mill has to say on any subject is that his intellectual credentials are overwhelmingly impressive. It is inconceivable that anyone would want to undergo the educational process that Mill experienced. It is also inconceivable that anyone by the time he was twenty was better educated than Mill. That one should receive training in the use of the mind is a concept that is the basis of all formal education. But probably no one has received that training to the extent that John Stuart Mill received it.

Yet Mill attended no school nor university, but was educated at home by his strict and exacting father, James, a disciple of Jeremy Bentham and one of the leading figures in the Utilitarian movement in England. James Mill believed that ordinary education fails to develop young people's intellectual capacity early enough. So he taught John, the oldest son, himself; and the son helped with the education of the other children of the family, nine in all. The extent of that education was staggering.

John started the study of Greek when he was three. By the time he was eight he had read in the original such Greek authors as Herodotus, Plato, Aesop, Xenophon, Lucius, Diogenes Laertius, and Isocrates. He studied algebra and the geometry of Euclid. Also, at eight he began the study of Latin and read the English historians Edward Gibbon and David Hume. At ten he could read Plato and Demosthenes with ease. At age twelve he undertook the serious study of scholastic logic and read

Aristotle's logical treatises in the original. By the time he was thirteen he had mastered the fundamentals of political economy, absorbing the ideas of Adam Smith and David Ricardo.

At age fourteen he was sent to France for a year of study, where he mastered the language, studied French culture and politics, and continued his study in economics. While in France he also studied Roman law, psychology, mathematics, chemistry, and botany.

Perhaps the justification for such an extensive review of a boy's education is that history presents us with no other case like it.

In 1823, at age seventeen, John joined the India House as a clerk in the examiner's office, which was headed up by his father. Rising rapidly through the ranks, John eventually succeeded his father as chief examiner. From 1836, thirteen years after his employment with the India House, until 1856, the year of his father's death, Mill had the responsibility of overseeing the India Company's relation with the Indian states.

In his first years with the company, he found time to write articles for the English newspapers, to assist his father on the "Westminster Review," and, before he turned twenty, to edit Bentham's *Treatise on Evidence*. During the entire period of his life, Mill was a contributor to practically every major British periodical, and even had experience as an editor. He was also active in debating societies and groups offering scheduled discussions, including the Utilitarian Society, which he founded, and the London Debating Society. The breadth and intensity of his thought was enormous, and he used his analytical skills to enhance the scope of English radicalism.

Mill was well aware that he was viewed by members of the London Debating Society as a "precocious phenomenon," a "made man," and an "intellectual machine." He was not impervious to such criticism, and it caused him to doubt the worth of an education that placed so little value on the emotional life of an individual, education so restricted that intimate relationship with others was discouraged. He was aware of an intense sense of loneliness which he felt could be satisfied only by a "perfect friendship." And, to make matters worse, there was no one he could discuss his misgivings with. For six months, in 1826-27, he hovered on the brink of despair, contemplating suicide. One day, while reading the memoirs of Marmontel, he came upon a passage that told of Marmontel's father's death, the plight of the family, and the sudden inspiration by which Marmontel would become everything to his family and provide for all its needs. Mill suddenly discovered in himself an emotion he had never before experienced, one which brought tears to his eyes, and a sudden sense of a new meaning for his life.

In 1830, Mill met the "perfect friend" who was to influence him more than anyone in his life except for his father. She was a married woman with children, who represented for Mill all of the desirable qualities lacking in himself. Harriet Taylor was twenty-three and Mill twenty-four when they met. She was a romantic who wrote poetry, was somewhat of a Bohemian and had "advanced" views on the subjects of love, marriage, divorce, and the status of women. And her views regarding the subject of liberty were remarkably compatible with Mill's own views. Both of them insisted that their relationship was strictly platonic, and Harriet cautioned Mill when he was writing his *Autobiography* to describe the relationship as one of "strong affection, intimacy of friendship, and no impropriety." But that is not what their acquaintances thought, nor was it was Harriet's husband thought, although Mill was able to work out a "reconciliation" with him.

The relationship, innocent as it might have seemed to them, caused them the loss of intimacy with family and friends. It was as though Walter Savage Landor's prescription should apply personally to them: "few acquaintances, fewer friends, no familiarities." Their "perfect friendship," lasted nearly twenty years, and it was not until two years after Mr. Taylor's death that they could consider marriage. Their marriage lasted seven years and ended with Harriet's death.

Both of them suffered periods of ill health, but they also suffered periods of self-imposed solitude. They severed almost all their relations with society, Mill finding it "insipid," lacking in serious discussion, harmful to the intellect, valued only by social climbers. This view was reflected in Mill's book *On Liberty* (and Harriet's, for he credits her with the inspiration for it as well as for actual statements in it). In the book can be found the exaltation of the individual and the distrust of conformity and social pressures which were a part of Mill's life at that time.

In 1865 he was elected a member of Parliament, giving him a stronger platform for his radical ideas. He was a strong supporter of the Reform Bill of 1867, but his causes also included the Irish land question, representation of women, and reduction of the national debt. He was consistently in favor of England's interfering in the affairs of other nations in cases where human freedom was involved.

In 1867 he was elected Rector of St. Andrew's University, a position he held for a single year. Also in 1867 Mill helped to establish England's first female suffrage society. His interests in women's rights was a natural extension of his liberal and humane spirit; his treatise titled *The Subjection of Women* was published in 1867. Women's subjugation was for Mill, not unlike the tyranny of the majority in a democratic society, an injustice to be addressed. And the same set of values which prompted him to advocate political *laissez-faire* policies, convinced him that women should be given the same opportunities for self-expression as men. Among the many enormously interesting things about John Stuart Mill is the fact that his significance for English-speaking people has nothing to do with his literary credentials.

The writings of Mill are required reading in many American colleges in our own time, just as they were required reading in English universities in Mill's time. But they were not and are not read as literature. Because Mill was so facile in providing new doctrines for consideration and the technical terminology required to support them, his work became immediately admired in English-speaking schools in many parts of the world. Of the important Victorian prose writers—and they were innumerable—Mill is the least literary. His analytic mind was concerned more with abstractions than with the concrete images of "literary" writers. His style tended to reflect his character—simple, honest, and direct. His manner was self-effacing and his style relatively colorless. And the fact that he was almost always lucid did not necessarily advance his cause, because he had a tendency to be lucid on both sides of the question under consideration.

Rather than presenting experiences for their own sake in the traditional literary mode, he generalized from experience. His whole education was designed to turn out an eighteenth century philosopher rather than a nineteenth century man of letters. And yet a knowledge of Mill is essential to our understanding of Victorian literature, just as a knowledge of Marx, Darwin, and Freud is essential to an understanding of so much of early twentieth century American literature.

There were in Mill's time people dedicated to what Thomas De Quincey called the "literature of power," in other words, literature that appealed to the emotions; and this literature was intended to exclude the "literature of knowledge," that which was designed to teach. Mill himself wrote no poetry, no fiction, and not much literary criticism. His strength does not lie in appealing to his readers' emotions. He did not have Macaulay's vitality and brilliance, nor Carlyle's fire and thunder, nor Ruskin's poetic gift for art criticism, nor Arnold's wit and sparkle. Still, lacking all these gifts, he remains one of the indispensable writers of the nineteenth century. His influence on the thought of his day is powerful. He continues to be read today, while some of his contemporaries who were more "literary" are not. Mill's *Autobiography* and *On Liberty* have been included in virtually every list of "Great Books" that has been drawn up since his death. His appeal is in the simplicity of his style, in its clarity, and in its apparent sincerity and conviction. He endures because of the quality , the image, and the significance of his ideas.

It is not always easy to pinpoint Mill's position on philosophical doctrines. He passed through stages—what he called "periods"—over the many years he wrestled with them. That was so partly because he examines meticulously a host of social, economic, moral, and philosophical issues, varying his position as reason and experience dictated. He was a major spokesman for the Utilitarian movement, yet was not himself a utilitarian in the classical sense. He advocates empiricism in his logic, but he acknowledged the value of deduction. He moved easily from one philosophical position to another, following most readily any line of reasoning that exhibited the least bit of relevance or promise of relevance. Nor was he immune to the attractions of the newly arrived Romantic Age.

It has been suggested that no matter how

eminent the "eminent Victorians" were they can have little to say to a generation a hundred years removed from them in time and light years in morals. The charge may apply to many of John Stuart Mill's contemporaries, men like Thomas Carlyle, Walter Pater, Matthew Arnold, John Ruskin, and Charles Kingsley. But how irrelevant can a person be who was once arrested for passing out birth control literature to the poor on the streets of London? And that was only one of the radical causes to which Mill was committed.

Like his father, James Mill, and Jeremy Bentham, the founder of Utilitarianism, John was deeply interested in economic, political, and social problems, which he discussed in some detail in his writings. They are found most cogently set forth in his classic *Principles of Political Economy*, his no less classic *On Liberty*, his *Thoughts on Parliamentary Reform,* and his *Views on Representative Government.* He was to follow this with *On the Subjection of Women*, his *Essays on Religion*, and his books on the philosophy of William Hamilton and Auguste Comte.

A thread of consistency runs through all of Mill's speculative work: he wanted to provide unquestionable methods of proof for the conclusions arrived at in the moral and social sciences. While Auguste Comte's positivism—the view that science yields sure belief where human life is concerned—had great influences on Mill, the greatest influence came from Isaac Newton, whose physics, proclaimed a hundred and fifty years before Comte, was accepted as a coherent model of scientific thought by such English empiricists as Locke, Hume, Bentham, and James Mill.

The significance of Mill's ideas is best exemplified in his three most influential works which earned him the greatest respect as well: *System of Logic, Principles of Political Economy*, and *On Liberty*; in fact, these passed through several editions in Mill's lifetime. And all three exhibit Mill's belief that freedom is of paramount importance in human affairs.

Mill's *System of Logic* appeared in 1843 in

two volumes and was an instant success. It quickly went through many editions and had a significant influence on logicians as diverse as John Venn and Bertrand Russell.

It is a mistake to conclude, as some have done, that John Stuart Mill's *Logic* is a rejection of Aristotle's method of deduction. Indeed, he defended Aristotle's syllogism against the Scottish philosophers who argued that "deduction" should be replaced by "induction." Mill's own view was that inductive logic should supplement, not replace deductive logic. It is true that Mill was influenced by empiricism and associationist psychology, and he believed that all correct methods of reasoning are inductive, that is, are provided by experience. Since induction leads to general rules to which the particulars have contributed, it was apparent to Mill that no conclusions could be drawn by way of deduction except what the particulars have already provided. But for Mill that was not sufficient reason to throw out the whole system of deductive logic.

The logic Mill was interested in providing was the logic of the human sciences–history, psychology, and sociology–which should be based on causal explanation in the manner put forth by David Hume, in the eighteenth century. Hume's position was that where cause and effect are concerned, we can never know cause. We can only know that two things occur together, one antecedently, the other consequently; or, they may simply arise simultaneously. Because of the uniformity of nature, we can not discount its laws. But "causation" can mean little more than uniformity.

For Mill, it was perfectly apparent that the social, moral, and economic ideal lies in the greatest amount of individual freedom and self expression compatible with the greatest good for the greatest number. This was, of course, the very definition of Utilitarianism; and, by the time he was twenty, Mill had become the chief spokesmen for the philosophical system created by Bentham and his father.

Mill's larger views of liberty, discussed so cogently in all his major works, are not linked solely to his distaste for anything that tended to destroy the freedom of the individual, such as paternalism, regimentation, and socialism. Nor are they founded on some vague notion of the value placed on freedom in advanced societies. They stemmed from his logic based view of free will and necessity.

Mill had resolved the question of free will and necessity by appealing to nature and the uniformities nature presents. Because of those uniformities we have been able to construct an exact and reliable body of knowledge which, as yet, is uncontradicted by the course of events. But the laws with which the physical sciences deal, particularly that of causation, reveal little more than nature's uniformity. However, necessity is not revealed in that uniformity. Causation rests on the observation of invariable antecedents and consequents as well as the assumption the same antecedents will yield the same consequents. But what comes after is not necessarily caused by what comes before. To connect events to necessity requires the detection of circumstances that precede a given event under *all* conditions. Necessity on this view means nothing more than unconditional sequence.

The upshot of all this is that free will becomes an adjunct of the natural world. Man, being a part of nature, is subject to her uniformities. His acts are determined by the interaction of character and environment. Knowing what someone is like makes it possible to predict what that person will do in given circumstances. All our dealings with our fellow human beings are based on the assumption of human uniformity no less than our reactions to the physical world are based on the observed uniformity of nature.

For Mill, then, there is as much necessity in human nature as there is in physical nature, but in neither case can we detect the compulsion. Our acting orderly does not deprive us of the feeling of liberty. We are the source of our actions, we have responsibility for them, we play an active role in forming our own characters. Our behavior is directed by our desires and ideals and "cause" us to be and do what we want. This is the essence of freedom.

To the question, "What are our desires and ideals?" Mill answers, Utilitarianism. Moral good is simply the greatest happiness for the greatest number, and happiness is pleasure. But at this point Mill departs from Bentham's "hedonistic calculus," based solely on quantitative criteria, such as the proximity, intensity, duration, purity, and like considerations, of the pleasure involved. For Mill some pleasures are intrinsically preferable to others simply because they are "higher" pleasures. Intellectual pleasures, for example, are preferable to sensual ones. No intelligent person, Mill thinks, would sacrifice his intelligence, even if he could be certain that if he were more stupid he would be more contented. Better, he said, to be a Socrates dissatisfied than a pig satisfied.

Then, too, where Bentham put the source of altruistic feelings as self-interest, Mill, not comfortable with the narrowness of this conception of human nature, thought that the social impulses lying behind the greatest good for the greatest number were of a primitive rather that a self-interested nature. In other words, people are naturally self sacrificing and altruistic. Individual happiness is best achieved by promoting the happiness of the group. Mill did believe, however, that altruism could be overdone, if one were to sacrifice one's own interests for the sake of others. These corrections of Bentham resulted in humanizing Utilitarianism in a way Bentham and James Mill would not have approved.

Mill believes that individual happiness is best achieved by promoting the happiness of the group. And he went on to insist that the greatest happiness for the greatest number could be attained only under the condition of the greatest possible individual freedom. It takes all kinds of people to create a world, and the more room that is provided in the world for self-development and individual expression, the better chance everyone has to be happy. This meant that room must be made for mankind's affections and emotions. Mill had come to realize that the lack of such considerations was a fatal flaw in Bentham's system. Bentham thought that poetry, for example, was an empty game, and Mill's own father would have agreed with Plato that poetry is an enemy of truth. Mill, however, saw it as valuable because of its therapeutic effect on human emotions.

Anyhow, what is important in all this is Mill's insistence that liberty is the basis for human happiness.

In dealing with the matter of political economy, Mill was less speculative and more historical. To a generation familiar with the names if not the theories of John Maynard Keynes and Kenneth J. Arrow it may seem surprising that the intricacies of political economy and its international ramifications had been examined in great detail two centuries earlier. The first work to lay out in any systematic way the framework of political economy was Adam Smith's *Wealth of Nations*, published in 1776. Marx's *Das Capital* soon followed, but neither of these works was even in a cursory way understood by the general reading public. Malthus added his more original theories and Ricardo his more

logical ones, but it remained for John Stuart Mill to sum up the discoveries of his predecessors and give them coherence in the minds of the general public. And that he did in his two volume work, *Principles of Political Economy*, in 1848.

The contrast between Smith's classic work and Mill's equally classic one has often been commented on. Both men were trained as philosophers but had a keen interest in political matters. Both believed that political and commercial activity could best be influenced by theory; but in reflecting on the motives for such theory each was given a broader understanding of the issues involved. But while Smith looked to the future, Mill looked to the past, viewing economics and politics as a philosophical historian. Smith had to prepare the public mind for his theories, while Mill's audience recognized them as the embodiment of accumulated human wisdom. Two generations of English statesmen had had an opportunity to put Smith's theories to the test—men like Canning and Huskisson, Cobden and Peel. And the testing of Smith's theories had resulted in strings of unrivaled legislative and economic successes. It was in this political and economic environment that Mill wrote his famous treatise.

Critics have suggested that there was a downside to all this—that these Victorians were so certain of everything they said and wrote, so heavily invested in the present that they paid no attention to the future. Thomas Macaulay was a perfect example of such an attitude. Lord Melbourne is said to have complained, "I only wish I was as cocksure of anything as Tom Macaulay is of *everything*."

The importance of Mill's *Principles of Political Economy* lay not so much in the discovery of new truths for generations to come, but in the revelation of present truths on which men of his generation were relying. As a record of the theories which inspired the political practices of the first half of the nineteenth century, Mill's work is, therefore, of monumental importance.

His conviction that the social institutions of a society were irrevocably linked to their economic practices led Mill to study the principles of socialism, which were attracting great attention throughout Europe, but he was himself not attracted to socialism as a system of government. On the other hand, he challenged some of the most cherished ideals of capitalism. He failed, for example, to see what was so sacred about the concept of private property. And he preferred to treat production and distribution as separate considerations. As a result he could not support distribution systems which put the working class at starvation levels.

If Mill's work on political economy fails to give an accurate analysis of human conduct, its importance as a historical document is incontestable. If it did not accurately describe the way people act, it is argued, it did provide a true picture of the way in which intelligent people in the middle of the nineteenth century thought they acted.

The economics of the Victorian Age were not, however, created by those who wrote books about the subject. The chief impetus came from the English statesmen who, in the first half of the eighteenth century, laid the foundation for the largest commercial empire the world had ever known. John Stuart Mill's father had been a leader in developing economic policies to fit the politics of the time, but it remained for his son to describe them more fully and accurately.

John Stuart Mill had been an active participant in the struggle which was to discard the error-ridden system of public charity, to bring about reform of the national currency, to establish free trade, and to develop a system of colonialism more enlightened and productive than any that had preceded it. Mill was, therefore, more than the historian of Britain's economic philosophy; he had helped to establish it, and his successes in helping to bring these reforms about were well known. It was undoubtedly the reputation of the man as much as the reputation of the book that resulted in his *Principles of Political Economy* being required reading at Oxford and Cambridge. Moreover, it was his greatness as a man that accounts for his greatness as a writer.

Few people of his era, men or women, have stood the test of time as well as Mill has. It has been said of him that he took institutions and principles existing in his own time and treated them as though they existed forever, but it was several years before his assumptions and conclusions came under attack. With Jevons and his followers came the idea that things should not be analyzed according to their supposed inherent utility, but how they affect man as a human being. But for many people today, Mill's treatise on political economy is valuable because it contains the practice-based conclusions of the pioneers of economic thought rather than the speculations of those who were to follow.

The most enduring aspect of Mill's legacy, the one which has had most appeal for the popular mind, is his work *On Liberty* which was published in 1859, the year that Darwin's *Origin of Species* appeared in print. It would be extremely difficult to conceive of two more radical books which had such instant appeal for the general public, nor two books which received such instant and harsh condemnation for the ideas they presented.

*On Liberty* does not attack the kinds of tyranny identified so clearly and consistently by the proponents of the American and French Revolutions. It is, rather, an attack on the tyranny of the majority in democratic societies. But Mill was mindful of the fact that in a democracy such as America the pressure for conformity always posed a threat to individualism—particularly intellectual individualism, which can least afford to be crushed—and reduce it to the level of what he called "collective mediocrity." Mill's enthusiasm for democratic government was always tempered by his realization that there is a wide difference between democratic ideals and democratic practices. He knew that if people were better, societies would be better. As citizens became better educated and wiser, he thought, the moral, social, and economic problems would justify less social interference and control. In all Mill's writings, even in his discussions, of what socialism has to offer, he is emphatic in his insistence that the individual is more important than institutions such as the state or the church.

Mill was, of course, only one of many to celebrate the cause of freedom. The Englishmen Milton and Locke had issued manifestos of a sort as early as the seventeenth century; Germaine de Staël had celebrated liberty in France; contemporaries—Adam Smith, Thomas Paine, America's Founding Fathers, Goodwin, Emerson, Thoreau, Proudhon, and Stirner—had all written eloquently in behalf of some aspect of liberty. But for Mill liberty was a sovereign principle against which the thoughts of individuals as well as the actions of individuals and society were to be tested.

Mill's approach to the issue of freedom is overly simplistic, chiefly because it rests on "one very simple principle," that individuals should have complete control over what they think, say, and do so long as they do not harm others. The difficulty here is that his "one very simple principle" cannot be applied without first answering a question implicit is his formulation of the principle: Who should decide which actions are harmful to society and should therefore be restricted. Mill doesn't answer the question, although he does say that the individual has jurisdiction over his "self-regarding" conduct, while society has jurisdiction over "other-regarding" conduct. The problem is in deciding what actions adversely affect other people—and the answers to that have never been satisfactorily supplied. Mill was as reluctant to put the responsibility for deciding the question on the individual as he was to put it on society. Whatever its virtues, Mill's principle offers no guidance in deciding the morality of "other-regarding" conduct.

In Mill's own time many people objected to his applying liberty to utilitarianism; but it wasn't utility that Mill was appealing to in trying to promote his "one very simple principle"—it was liberty itself as a sovereign principle, and one that was based on happiness as a natural product of liberty.

It was objected, too, that Mill, by insisting on liberty and individuality, tended to make truth subservient to both, at least in one sense, that an adversarial position was necessary, even in cases where the accepted opinion was entirely true and the dissenting opinion entirely false. If the utility of truth is the basis for its acceptance, then, obviously, liberty, not truth, is the paramount principle.

And when liberty of action is taken into account, Mill's argument for it is consistent with that which he advances for the liberty of thought and discussion. But, it is pointed out, instead of truth being victorious, all kinds of things people value might win out—goods not seen as necessarily beneficial to society. For example, "eccentricity, peculiarity, spontaneity, originality, variety, diversity, impulse, passion, experiments in living could come at the expense of conformity, obedience, restraint, discipline, custom, tradition, public opinion, and social pressure," the latter group being seen as more conducive to the well being of society.

Most critics of Mill—and they were numerous—did not agree with Mill that the decline of individuality could turn England into another China. They did not think that conformity was that great or eccentricity that rare in England. Other critics argued that if cohesiveness of a society was achieved by shared ideas and fewer social types, then society had a responsibility to concern itself with the affairs of individuals.

Macaulay, Carlyle, and Newman all voiced strong objections to Mill's view of liberty; but perhaps the strongest and most generally accepted was that presented by James Stephen, who argued that liberty was in itself no more desirable than fire. Time, place, and circumstance all figured into determining the value to be placed on it. Society, said Stephen, had the right to use all means at its disposal to protect its interests. Progress of societies, he maintained, is dependent upon moral, legal, and religious coercion. If you accepted Mill's argument, said Stephen, society would not have the ability to take the action necessary to protect itself whenever the need arose. Besides, the withholding of sanctions against a particular belief or act would amount to giving approval of it or sanction for it.

Present-day critics have even more to say against Mill's "one very simple principle." While Mill recognized the difference between moral and immoral acts, and while he would not approve of punishment for private immoral acts, he still recognized them as immoral. But his critics complain that building an atmosphere of neutrality where individualism was concerned is tantamount to fostering moral relativism; so then not only does social interference become questionable, but moral judgment as well. Mill himself was not a moral relativist, but his case for social neutrality made him sometimes appear like one. He knew that liberty did not vacate responsibility. That is why the qualification for the "one very simple principle" is so important. That there must be responsibility for ideas as there is for actions is a point Mill does not dwell at length on.

If *On Liberty* is not required reading as his Logic and *Principles of Political Economy* were, it has been suggested by one of the leading authorities on Mill that the book has "by process of cultural assimilation" become a gospel of the present age even more than it was in Mill's day. And in spite of all the objections that can be raised against the principles of liberty, such as insisting that the elevation of the idea of liberty leads to the debasement of authority, it remains the only moral principle to which the Western world gives general assent—in principle, if not in practice.

What Mill will always be remembered and valued for is the purity of his motives, the rigor of his thinking, the energy and independence with which he addressed his ideals, and for the effect his ideas had not only on those with whom he came into contact, personally and as a writer, but on the whole intellectual and moral life of his time.

GALILEO

BY
JERRY
ANDERSON

# *Galileo Galilei*
## 1564-1642

*"Philosophy is written in the vast book which stands open before our eyes, I mean the universe; but it cannot be read until we have learnt the language and become familiar with the characters in which it is written."*

It is inconceivable that anyone taking a high school or college course in physics could escape being introduced to Galileo, the father of experimental mechanics, the most influential scientist since Aristotle, and the first effectually to use the telescope to study the skies.

Students learn that Galileo discovered the isochronism of the pendulum (in his first year at the university). He went on to invent the hydrostatic balance, the proportional compass, and an elementary form of air thermometer. He discovered the law of uniform acceleration, the trajectory of projectiles, the principle of virtual velocities, the dynamics of impact, the specific gravity of air; and he experimented with acoustics, light, and magnetism. Galileo also made important improvements in the construction and use of the telescope and the microscope.

It was Galileo's work with the telescope that brought him into conflict with the Catholic Church. That work was not inconsiderable. His astronomical observations in 1609-1610 include the mountains on the moon, the collection of stars making up the Milky Way, Saturn, the satellites of Jupiter, spots on the sun, and the phases of Venus. His initial observations were set forth in his first book, the Sidereus Nuncius, in 1610.

But any meaningful account of Galileo must deal not so much with the specific inventions and discoveries of this remarkable man, but the fractured culture in which he lived and the forces that shaped his mind and drew out his genius.

Galileo was born into a Renaissance world in which all kinds of changes in thought and character were taking place. Intellectual interests had broken the hold of theology on men's minds. The desire to gain knowledge found its expression in many different ways—in the discovery of ancient texts, in the discovery of new lands and customs, and in the discovery that man himself was an uncharted land.

A review of science, technology, and philosophy in Galileo's time gives a striking picture of Galileo's contributions to the modern world. He is better known to the non-scientific public for his alleged experiments with falling bodies from the top of the Tower of Pisa than for his exploits with the telescope—better known, that is, as a physicist than as an astronomer; and it is as a physicist that he made his greatest contribution to the history of human thought.

Galileo belonged to a culture in rapid transition from the Renaissance to the Scientific Age. He was, in fact, the world's first scientist who used mathematical data to support his conclusions. Because he stood at the crossroads of history, attempts to view him as ushering in the scientific age without regard to the ancient and medieval influences upon which he was to act and against which he was to react do much to distort the essential features of his greatness. To understand Galileo as a man as well as a scientist, one must look to Galileo's past, a past that contained the best that the Italian Renaissance could offer. It will prove useful to look at the times *into* which he was born before noting the time *at* which he was born.

Galileo is not generally recognized by his family name, Galilei. Not many people in the lists of famous men and women are referred to by their first names, and Galileo was among the last to have that distinction. But it is well observed that Galileo was not born into a family so much as into a tradition. And that tradition marked the very essence of Italy during the Renaissance.

Being a citizen of Florence during the Renaissance was to share a certain well defined social, cultural, and religious environment. But, with all the benefits, there went obligations. Being born in the city of Florence or taking up residence there did not make one a "citizen." Only families whose members had served in city government could lay claim to the title. Galileo was born in Pisa, not Florence, but still he could claim the title of "citizen" because his father, a merchant and a prominent musician, was a descendant of a citizen. As a result, Galileo could claim a share in the moral, intellectual, artistic, and physical treasures of the city, of which there appeared to be an illimitable number. Florence boasted an unbroken chain of geniuses, from Giotto to Michelangelo in art, and from Dante to Ariosto in literature. The neoplatonist sympathies of the educated class in Florence would encourage Galileo to honor the Platonic precepts of truth, goodness, and beauty which were revealed by Florence's priceless masterpieces.

But when Galileo was born, the power of the Catholic Church was supreme, with the clergy imposing its influence through the unbridled fanaticism of the Inquisition.

The correspondence of Galileo's personality to the portrait of the Florentine citizen has been admirably noted by Giorgio Spini: "His manly realism, his love of an active, and of anything useful and concretely practical; his typically Florentine irony and his high opinion and masterly use of the Volgare [Italian language]; his enthusiasm for poetry, music, fine arts in general, and for Dante and Michelangelo in particular; his strong humanistic background, his fondness for Plato, and his exalted conception of man's intellectual dignity, so near to that of the fifteenth century Florentine Neoplatonists."

It is true that Galileo never married but took as a mistress a Venetian woman by whom he had two sons and a daughter. He took Marina Goumba as a mistress for the same reason that all men who take women as mistresses do so. She was no Laura, it is argued, who inspired Dante's Platonic sense of love; she was no Beatrice who inspired Petrarch's "high style"; and she was no Vittoria Colonna who helped Michelangelo reach the high levels of idealism expressed in his religious art. Galileo knew love only in the physical sense, and that was good enough for him.

When he left Padua to return to Florence, in deference it is said, to the moral sentiment of the city that nurtured him, he left Marina behind.

Galileo's biographers have pointed out the lack of Florentine idealism in Galileo. Even though he loved and was highly competent in music and the fine arts, he did not moralize, or attempt to discover philosophical and religious messages in the arts which he loved and studied. Even in his critical pieces on Tasso and Ariosto, it has been pointed out, he is purely literary—there is no looking for nuances of meaning. His early piece on Dante's *Inferno*, as competent as it is in logic, technical skill, and handling of the Italian tongue, makes no reference to Dante's ideals or contains any suggestion that an Inferno even exists.

It has been suggested that Galileo's choice of Italian for the greatest part of his writings was based on his desire to find, like Dante, a new class of readers. Rather than address himself, as Kepler did, to a specialized audience, he wrote as a philosopher addressing the common man. "The reason which moves me," Galileo wrote, "is the sight of the young going off indifferently to study to be philosophers, doctors, or whatever, many of them being inadept, while others, who could be capable, remain at home or in occupations alien to literature."

Did literature play a part in his life? Was it an escape from his preoccupation with science, or was it related more vitally to his scientific work? By one account, his treatment of Tasso suggests that it is not the rational scientist that influences the critic, but the literary man in Galileo that influences the astronomer; and that while he might accept the idea that poetry would follow the path laid out by Tasso, he recognized the necessity for separation of the fields of knowledge, and the need to establish a language of experience.

Galileo's talents were extraordinarily varied. He was an accomplished artist, winning praise from several notable painters of his time. He once considered painting as a career. He was also well versed in music (a special interest of his father); he played the lute. As a writer, while not great, he was competent. He had an intense love for the poets of his country and is said to have memorized Ariosto by heart.

Galileo was born February 15, 1564 at Pisa, a date notable because it was the day that Michelangelo died, and the year that

Shakespeare was born. Pisa was at that time under the government of the Medicis of Florence, though earlier it had been a free city. Galileo's father was an impoverished nobleman, a merchant, with a love for music and mathematics and a reputation for being quarrelsome and obstinate.

Galileo's early studies in the University of Pisa were in the field of medicine. The study of medicine in all of Europe in those days was much like the study of law in England at a later time: it was a study which would occupy a young man's attention until a suitable profession could be found for him. The young Galileo, however, was much more attracted to exact sciences, and there was nothing very exact about medicine in those days. It is said that he used to listen to the lectures on mathematics at the door of the classroom, and then ask questions of the students as they left. This interest soon got Galileo enrolled in mathematics, and, by the time he was twenty-five, he became lecturer in that subject at the university in his home town of Pisa.

Galileo's rejection of Aristotelian physics made him unpopular with the faculty, which had no great admiration for or attraction to independent thought. His experiments with free-falling bodies is associated with his four-year stay at Pisa. A legend now rejected has it that he angered his colleagues when he dropped three objects of different weights from the Leaning Tower of Pisa and showed, from their striking the ground at the same time, that Aristotle was wrong in his theory that the velocity of falling bodies varied with their weights. One reason for rejecting this experiment as factual is that the Flemish mathematician Stevin had carried out the experiment before Galileo at another place; so there would have been no reason for Galileo to repeat it.

In 1592 Galileo was offered a position at the University of Padua by the Senate of Venice. He remained at that post for twenty years, lecturing and writing chiefly in Italian rather than in Latin. After writing his *Sidereus Nuncius*, Galileo gave up the use of Latin, the language of the university and the Church, and wrote for the people in their own tongue—writing, he said, for those who had eyes to see and minds to understand. Besides, the professors and the clerics were those who were least receptive to his ideas. Another reason for choosing Italian may be attributed in part to his love of literature. After all, the great writers of Italy in the Middle Ages—Dante, Petrarch, and Boccaccio—all chose to write in the native tongue.

The scientific background of Galileo's thought and work is as compelling in many ways as the cultural background of Renaissance Florence. Ernest Moody has pointed out that Ernst Mach, in his treatise on the science of mechanics, published in 1869, asserts unequivocally that dynamics was founded by Galileo. In the case of free fall, according to Mach, no knowledge of the subject existed before Galileo's time, and Galileo had to create these ideas and the means to verify them. But, soon after Mach's work appeared, the *Notebooks* of Leonardo de Vinci were published, and it was clear that Leonardo had approached the problems of dynamics in ways very similar to the way they were approached by Galileo. Even as early as 533 AD, a man named James Philoponus had discovered that two objects of vastly different weights would fall at about the same rate of time.

An interesting account of Galileo's indebtedness to fourteenth century natural philosophy (if not science) is expressed by what is called "Duhem's Thesis." It is cited as a matter of record that Duhem, a Frenchman, looking for the source of Galileo's information on mechanics by examining the bibliographies in Leonardo's time, discovered that many of the texts were written by teachers of natural philosophy in Paris and Oxford during the 1300's.

Duhem concluded that these fourteenth

century scholastics had formulated a theory of mechanics quite different from that advanced by Aristotle and amazingly similar to that employed by Galileo and his contemporaries. For example, it is pointed out, that "laws" concerning the motion of projectiles and gravitation, which involve the law of inertia and the concept of force, were first suggested by a scholar named John Buridan of Paris in the fourteenth century. Buridan's ideas were passed on to Galileo by way of Buridan's pupil Albert of Saxony. Galileo then expressed the laws mathematically.

Duhem believed that Galileo had inherited a newly-formed scientific expression of the late Middle Ages, and he had done so at a time when Renaissance scholars had rejected the medieval tradition and had placed the science of Aristotle once again in a pre-eminent position in the Italian universities. It is not, said Duhem, the victory of a young modern science over medieval philosophy that Galileo demonstrates, but the triumph of fourteenth century science, born at Paris, over the views of Aristotle and Averroës.

What Galileo presented as an "impetus" theory of dynamics in his early work *De Motu* is a more exact rendering of the general dynamic theory formulated by the fourteenth century scholastics. And, it is argued, Galileo still deserves credit as the originator of modern classical dynamics. This is because Galileo did what his fourteenth century predecessors did not do. He built up a science of mechanics on the foundation of mathematics, whereas they saw no need of measuring concurrent variations and establishing and testing laws of motion.

Was there such a thing as a fourteenth century science of mechanics? The answer is, clearly, yes. Was Galileo influenced by the interpretation given of it at Paris and Oxford? The answer again is yes, although how he came by a knowledge of it is unknown. It is generally conceded, however, that what the medieval scholastics were doing was more of an attempt to refute Aristotle than to ground their theories on irrefutable evidence as Galileo had done. Nor was this attempt to refute Aristotle limited to medieval scholars of the fourteenth century. It was expressed also by Aristotle's successors in Alexandria and by Latin scholars, Muslims, and others, long before Leonardo expressed his views.

And what was there in Aristotle's theory of mechanics to refute? One idea had to do with what is called "projectile motion." Aristotle had argued that when a stone is thrown into the air something in contact with it was necessary to keep it in motion, and that could not be the hand of the thrower. Aristotle's theory was that the propulsion of air in contact with the stone kept the stone in motion. In the descent phase, the motion of free-fall was involved.

Not liking Aristotle's account of motion, others suggested what is called the "impressed power" theory or "impetus" theory. This holds that the force imparted by the hand of the thrower impresses on the stone a power to continue in motion until the power is overcome by gravity and the stone falls with increasing speed.

Undoubtedly Galileo was familiar with ideas being formulated in the fourteenth century, but it is not at all clear that he thought himself indebted to them in any substantial way. He does show in the *Dialogues* and *Discourses* that he was aware of the mechanical theory put forth by his predecessors; and, it has been suggested, he believed his predecessors had looked for proof but failed to find it. He believed, and rightly so, that he was the first to demonstrate that in the free-fall of bodies the distances traveled increase with the square of the times. But even he, like his predecessors, had early in his career mistakably believed that the increase in velocity was a function of distance rather than of time.

It would be a mistake, then, to believe that Galileo was the first to postulate a theory of mechanics, but it is in providing a mathematical model for his theories that Galileo helped to establish mechanics as a science. Put another way, Galileo was the first modern natural philosopher with the eyes of a mathematical physicist, seeing mathematics in every motion of every natural object.

When Galileo is credited with being the father of modern science, it is not because he established new facts. What makes Galileo the father of modern science—or more precisely, the father of modern physics—is his method of inquiry, his insistence that truth be tested by observation and experiment. He was attracted to experiments that were capable of being quantitatively expressed, such as constructed pendula or tilted planes, where he could control the length of the lamp or the acceleration of the falling body at will. To refer to him as the father of experimental science is simply to recognize his primacy in the use of laboratory measurement, of experimental controls, of repeated measurements, and careful recording of the data which he viewed with the eyes of a mathematical physicist.

**M**any scientists have recognized in Galileo a strain of the theoretical scientist, one who foresaw the result of an experiment before conducting it, with his experiments carried out to convince others more than to convince himself. Galileo's experiments in the mechanics of physical bodies is legendary, yet it has been argued that he was not a great experimentalist in a typical repetitive data-gathering sense. With respect to his Law of Inertia, for example, he theorized that if two inclined planes were located at opposite ends of a room, and a sphere were allowed to roll down one plane, it would, in the absence of friction, travel up the second plane to the height at which it had been released on the first plane. Experimentation would only demonstrate what he had already known—that the driving force of the descent of a sphere was equal to the driving force of its ascent.

Galileo's genius lay in his ability to reveal the truth of dynamics in the language of mathematics, and he did this with the style and grace of an artist. It was that which revealed him to be "the conceptual master of nature." But another feature of his genius lay in abstracting a problem from its experimental grounds by saying what would happen to a body if its environment were neutralized, standardized, or eliminated. Whereas Aristotle believed that the activity of a body in its natural state could be understood only by observation, Galileo believed that he could account for the laws of motion by the application of the mind alone. Like Plato, he claimed that "the book of nature is to be read only in mathematical characters," intending to suggest that objects capable of being described in terms of numbers, weight, etc., could provide the direction that deductive reasoning would take, just as numbers did for mathematicians, especially for those who practiced geometry.

But the problem was that the "book of nature" was capable of being read in ways quite contrary to beliefs held by the Roman Catholic Church. For centuries it was recognized that God revealed himself in his work as well as in his word, but it was never considered a possibility that the work might contradict the word—not only the word revealed in the Bible, but the doctrines that had been hammered out in church council after council to supplement the word. It was also never considered that reason would be employed in any way other than as a

handmaid to faith; and if church doctrine flew in the face of God-given reason and the God-given senses, what then?

In a way Galileo could convince himself that his philosophy did not run contrary to Christian dogma. Plato, after all, had been embraced by the Church just as Aristotle had been, but in a non-scientific way. Plato's theory of inborn ideas could be used to support the view that, in reading the book of nature written by the creator in mathematical language, one simply discovers the truth already in his mind.

For hundreds of years prior to Galileo's time, man's thinking in Europe was controlled by the dogma and authority of the Roman Catholic Church. Since Galileo's time, science and authority have not been comfortable bedfellows. But, it has been said, "the battle is one that science can never finally win. The deep-seated habits of laziness are too universal. The overwhelming majority of people wish to be told what to think."

This rather pessimistic picture of the progress of truth gives a rather one-sided picture. It is not as though dogma and authority were, in themselves, the forces of evil with which science must contend; and nowhere is that more evident than in Galileo's own case. When, in 1543 Copernicus, of Poland, published his theory that the sun, not the earth, is the center of the solar system, Copernicus, who, was himself a canon of the Church, did not bring down on his head the fury of the ecclesiastical authorities, because his views were seen only as hypotheses. Actually, Copernicus had finished his work as early as 1530. In 1543, as he lay dying, a copy of his book was laid in his lap—with a preface supplied by an anonymous and officious cleric, hinting that the work should be viewed only as a hypothetical view of the solar system.

When Galileo was summoned to Rome in 1633, the Copernican heliocentric theory was almost a hundred years old. It had caused no real heartburn for the Catholic Church in its first half century because it did not assert anything as truth. Besides, in its hundred years it had won relatively few adherents. The common man had no real understanding of it. The professors and the clerics had three good reasons for ignoring it: First, it was contrary to precepts embedded in the philosophic tradition of the Western world; second, it negated church doctrine; and, third, it flew in the face of common sense.

This latter reason was probably the most compelling of all, particularly when applied to that part of Copernican theory that holds that the earth moves. The idea that the earth turns daily on its axis (only one of its movements) was patently absurd. Not only did common sense tell us that the earth is stationary, but it could be confirmed by observation. If a stone were dropped from a tower on earth, moving from east to west on its axis (because the earth, was said to move in that direction), then the stone would hit the earth well to the west of the tower; and experience showed that the stone falls vertically. Galileo eventually solved that problem by proposing a new theory of motion.

*I*t is argued that Galileo had the misfortune to champion Copernicanism at a time when the Catholic Church, after more than a half a century of neutrality, decided to crush it. That view gives the appearance of placing Galileo in the wrong place at the wrong time. A more accurate appraisal might be that it was Galileo's unrelenting attack on Aristotleianism and his gradual commitment to the Copernican theory as truth rather than as hypothesis that earned him the wrath of the Inquisition. It was his early discoveries with the telescope as recorded in his *Sidereus Nuncius* that won him over to the Copernican position. In the 1590's, as a professor at Padua, he had taught the Ptolemaic (geocentric) theory of the cosmos, but he was to confide in a letter to Kepler in 1597 that he had "become a convert to the opinion of Copernicus many years ago." With his astronomical discoveries, his defense of the Copernican doctrine became more pronounced; and, with the discovery of the moons of Jupiter and the phases of Venus, his commitment to Copernicanism was complete.

Galileo's work with the telescope did not begin until 1609. That year, while in Venice, he learned of experiments by Dutch scholars with magnifying glasses. Turning his attention to the phenomenon, he produced a telescope capable of a 3X magnification. By the time he had discovered the mountains on the moon he had 20X power, and eventually he achieved about 33X. The telescope was not suitable for scanning the skies until Galileo had discovered a method for shaping the lenses and determining the ratio of the focal lengths. In 1611, a year after publishing his *Sidereus Nuncius*, he traveled to Rome where he demonstrated his telescope to church authorities. The trouble started when he argued that Copernican doctrine could be reconciled with scriptures.

But Galileo, it should be remembered, lived at a time when a challenge to church doctrine was a rare event. Giordano Bruno had been burned at the stake for his astronomical and other heretical views as recently as 1600. Luther and Calvin had challenged the Church on ecclesiastical grounds, and radical views about nature were finding their way into Italy's universities. The response of the Church against this wave of heretical opinions was to launch the movement which has come to be known as the Counter-Reformation, from which emerged the Jesuits, an order of the Church dedicated to support this new movement. It was well known that Italy in Galileo's time had a reputation as a hotbed of hereticism and atheism, and actions to suppress both were deemed necessary.

A part of Galileo's problem was that he could not write for physicists because there were none. Physics before Galileo was treated as a branch of Aristotelian philosophy, not as an experimental science.

From the standpoint of the Church, Galileo had presented a cosmology diametrically opposed to that worked out by his predecessors and accepted by the Church.

In 1613, Galileo published his *Letters on Sunspots*, refuting a German philosopher named Scheiner. In this treatise Galileo comes out for Copernicus for the first time in print. His critics were furious. The first attack from the ecclesiastics was delivered from a pulpit in Florence in 1614. Galileo's response came in his *Letter to the Grand Duchess Christine of Lorraine*. There he recalled the words of Cardinal Baronius, which he agreed with: the "Holy Spirit intended to teach us in the Bible how to go to Heaven, not how the heavens go." The letter found its way to the Inquisition, and Galileo was warned by a cleric in Rome, "You can write as a mathematician and hypothetically as Copernicus is said to have done, and you can write freely as long as you keep out of the sacristy." The pope himself had told Galileo, "Surrender to the inscrutable, speculate as you like, but do not believe that we can really know." Galileo had traveled to Rome to argue openly for the Copernican theory, but he angered Pope Paul V, who appointed a church commission to examine the theory of the earth's motion.

Early in 1616, the Holy Office condemned

two propositions of Copernicus that Galileo had included in his *Letters on Sunspots*; Galileo was summoned before the Commissary of the Inquisition. Pope Paul V instructed Cardinal Bellarmine to admonish Galileo to abandon the Copernican theory. If he were to resist the admonition, and were to continue to teach Copernicanism orally or in writing, he would face imprisonment or worse. Galileo did not resist, but the Commissary of the Inquisition added the Pope's threat anyway—for good measure. Galileo was able to secure from the Cardinal a written statement saying that he had not been made to forsake his opinions nor compelled to perform penance. While he was cleared of unorthodoxy at that hearing, he was instructed not "to hold or defend" the Copernican theory.

In 1619, a controversy arose over the appearance of three comets. A Jesuit in Rome, Orazio Grassi, attempted to place them in the terrestrial sphere, since the celestial spheres were made up of a solid crystalline substance which carried the planets as they moved. Comets, obviously, could not move through solid spheres. Galileo replied with characteristic sarcasm through one of his students, but Grassi responded by attacking Galileo directly and accusing him of still holding the Copernican view. Galileo's extended response was contained in a book, the *Assayer*, which came out in 1623. In the book, couched in biting, sarcastic language, Galileo presented the principles which should guide scientific investigation, but he avoided giving support to Copernicus. What he did do was point out that new astronomical discoveries were more compatible with the Copernican than with the Ptolemaic system. In his trenchant manner, he suggested that since the first system was condemned by the Church and the second by reason, a third system would have to be discovered. Because Galileo's old friend and former pupil, Maffeo Barberius, was elected Pope about the time the *Assayer* was being printed, Galileo dedicated the book to him. The pope, who had taken the name Urban VIII, greatly enjoyed it; and it was well received in both scientific and ecclesiastical circles. Over a period of two months, Galileo had six audiences with the pope.

In 1624, Galileo was again in Rome, trying to persuade the pope to rescind the edict of 1616. The pope would not, but he gave Galileo permission to write a book comparing the old and the new systems, provided both were dealt with as hypotheses and without partiality. So far as the pope was concerned, it was to be nothing more than a hypotheses based on a single mathematical model. And the pope dictated to Galileo that the conclusion of his piece would be that God could have produced the same observable effects in an infinitely number of ways.

When, in 1632, Galileo's *Dialogues Concerning the Two Chief World Systems* appeared, it was an instant success. With his strong Platonic bias, Galileo employed the dialogue as the foremost method of instruction. It was clear, though, that it was not expressed in hypothetical language, nor was it impartial. It was strongly biased in favor of Copernicus. Five months later Galileo was summoned once more before the Inquisition. The pope, who had once been his friend, was now his enemy. The injunction of 1616 (now suspected to be a forgery) was resurrected and used against him. Galileo was forced to publicly withdraw his support for Copernicus, and was sentenced to life imprisonment. Because of Galileo's age and health, he was allowed to serve his confinement under house arrest in a villa outside Florence.

*I*solated and eventually blind, Galileo continued his work. His *Dialogue of the Two New Sciences* was smuggled out of Italy and printed in 1638. The book was based on the kind of scientific work he did in his youth and was considered by Galileo to be "superior to everything else of mine hitherto published." It would be his greatest contribution to science, and, together with his *Dialogue Concerning the Two Chief World Systems*, it would earn him universal respect. The books are of particular importance, when considering Galileo's impact on the history of ideas, in helping to distinguish between Galileo the symbol and Galileo the scientist.

Hardly less important than what he discovered is the way he expressed it. His writing is described as revealing "an ancient ecumenic and conciliatory spirit of Christendom with its rights and its freedoms"—a reference to his commitment to "all that was established in law and custom."

Galileo's greatness of character and his intellectual honesty and devotion to the truth attracted admirers by the thousands, and made him, more than any other man of his historical period, a highly cherished symbol of the best that the Renaissance mind had to offer.

He died in 1642, the year that Isaac Newton was born.

NEWTON

BY

JERRY

ANDERSON

# *Isaac Newton*
## 1643-1727

"*To myself I seem to have been only like a boy playing on the seashore, and diverting myself in now and then finding a smoother pebble or a prettier shell than ordinary, while the great ocean of truth lay all undiscovered before me.*"

To take the measure of a man whose contributions to science are almost without equal is a formidable task at best. To attempt to do so in a few pages about him is most intimidating, especially when that man is Isaac Newton.

One of the most respected biographers of Newton, Richard Westfall, found that the result of his twenty-year study of Newton served only to convince him that with Newton there is no measure—he is simply incomparable. He became for Westfall "one of a tiny handful of supreme geniuses who have shaped the human intellect." Einstein, who credited Newton for launching him on the road to his discovery of relativity, said of Newton, "Nature to him was an open book, whose letters he would read without effort."

A review of Newton's life and work reveals a person of complex thought and feeling. As professor Andrade has pointed out, Newton was of the world, and yet not of it. He was a supreme practitioner of the exact sciences, yet he was at heart a mystic. He was high-minded in his principles, yet he could be petty and quarrelsome in his dealings with friends as well as perceived enemies. He was a modest man, but could be overbearing. He was suspicious, sensitive, and shrinking, yet effective in conducting public affairs. He was capable of arousing admiration, respect, even reverence, yet seemed incapable of warm human affection. He mixed readily with people, especially after his move to London, yet he remained withdrawn, reluctantly yielding the secrets he had guarded all his life.

Because Newton's career was full of so many beginnings and cessations, with periods of complete abandonment from scientific studies, it is not particularly helpful to approach him chronologically. A more meaningful way of presenting him will be to look first at science as Newton inherited it, then at the reputation he enjoys, at some significant incidents in his career, at his writings of both a scientific and a nonscientific type, and, finally, at his two principle works for an appreciation of their importance.

Westfall's extraordinarily high opinion of Newton is shared by those who know him best— the members of the scientific community. In his lifetime, Newton published only two major works, the *Principia* and the *Opticks*. The *Principia* is considered by most men of science to be the greatest scientific book ever written, one of the most prodigious feats of the human intellect. Newton's importance can be appreciated by considering that the world after the publication of the *Principia* was never again seen in the same way his predecessors viewed it.

Moreover, because of the universal significance of his discovery of universal gravitation, it is argued that the quality of human thought was changed as was human experience itself. Of the *Opticks* it has been asserted that as a record of experiment and deduction from experiment, it reigns supreme. But, it is in the *Principia*, a shortened title of *The Mathematical Principles of Natural Philosophy* that Newton set forth his ideas about the motion of celestial bodies and universal gravitation.

One of the most remarkable incidents in the history of science is the rapid progress of astronomy in the hundred-and-fifty-year period from Copernicus to Newton (1530-1684). Between Copernicus' revolutionary idea that the earth was a small planet in the solar system, and Newton's conception of gravity as the force that holds the universe together, there appeared significant contributions by Kepler, Brahe, and Galileo. There was a marvelous degree of cooperation among those five principle investigators of the new cosmology, and it is not wholly insignificant that all five of them were of different nationalities. Newton's great contribution was his selective combination of the work of his predecessors—known today as the Newtonian Synthesis. It remains the most significant achievement of his life.

Not everyone, of course, believed in the geocentric theory of the universe developed by Ptolemy, with its cycles and epicycles accounting for the motions of celestial bodies observed from earth. Still, no serious movement to displace that system was made for fifteen hundred years; and it is a remarkable departure from the Ptolemaic system to that of Copernicus, who argued that not only was the earth simply a planet in the solar system, but that it moved.

It was in the treatment of motion that Newton made one of his greatest contributions. By his time, the scientific community was substantially in agreement about René Descartes' qualitative dualism—that is, that there are two things in the universe qualitatively distinct from one another—matter which moves and mind which thinks. Scientists disregarded the latter and concentrated on the former—matter (atoms) in motion. Newton's breathtaking accomplishment lay in his conviction that the whole physical universe is subject to the same law of gravitation and the same laws of motion. In his search for a mechanical explanation for the motion of the planets, he hit on gravitation as the glue that held the universe together. He took the name from the Latin word "gravitas," which means "weight," or "heaviness."

Until the seventeenth century, knowledge was considered to be largely the product of pure thought; and the thinker most respected in the western world was Aristotle. His encyclopedic writings, which had been preserved by the Arabs, were translated into Latin between 1200 and 1225, and were read with great enthusiasm by scholars throughout Europe. But new knowledge was almost always approached in a way that discounted observation and experimentation. So, instead of asking, "How does light express itself?" the philosophers would ask, "What is the nature of light?"—a completely different kind of question.

It might well be that the powers of deduction by men like Galileo, Newton, and Einstein make induction secondary. All three men had an almost uncanny power of perceiving scientific truths before they proved them. It has been said that Newton's pre-eminence was due to his ability to employ the "muscles of his intuition," which were "the strongest and most enduring with which a man has ever been gifted." He had the rare ability of holding a mental problem in his mind until he had "seen straight through it."

Even the most superficial review of Newton's life and works makes it abundantly clear that Newton possessed one of the greatest minds that science has produced; and perhaps no one has captured the majesty of that mind more eloquently than Wordsworth, who speaks of "Newton with his prism and his silent face," and "his mind forever voyaging through strange seas of thought alone."

One of the most compressed and satisfying summaries of Newton's importance reads as follows: "His brilliant and revolutionary contribution to science explained the working of a large part of inanimate nature in mathematical terms and suggested that the remainder might be understood in a similar fashion. By taking known facts, forming a theory that explained them in mathematical terms, deducing consequences from the theory, and comparing the results with the observed and experimental facts, he united for the first time the explanation of physical phenomena with the means of prediction—in the process converting physics from mere science of exploration into a general mathematical system."

Little wonder, then, that Newton is sometimes described as one of the greatest names in human thought, a supreme genius. The originality, scope, and importance of his contributions of the law of universal gravitation, the establishment of the fundamental features of physical optics, and the invention of the calculus resulted in the synthesis of all known facts concerning the physical universe. His powers of scientific intuition and deduction surpassed those of any other man of his time.

One of the remarkable things about Newton is the fact that he was much more than a mathematician, a physicist, and an astronomer. He also possessed to an admirable degree the intellectual aptitude of lawyer, historian, and theologian; and the writings he has left regarding those latter subjects are as extensive as they are impressive.

Newton's life was as long as it was illustrious, surprising because he was such a small, delicate child when he was born on Christmas day in 1642, that he was not expected to live. His father died before he was born, and his mother remarried when he was about two, turning him over to his maternal grandmother to raise. His mother never lost her affection for her son, and she returned to him after the death of her second husband. Of great importance, however, is the village in which Newton was born–Woolsthorpe, located about sixty miles north of London–because it was here his genius would flourish. While he was still very young, Newton attended the local school at Woolsthorpe; but at age eleven he entered the King's School in Grantham, a larger village a few miles away. His mother wanted him to farm the land, but his uncle and schoolmaster convinced her that the young Newton displayed a talent too great to be denied. Thus, after a couple of years on the family farm, at age seventeen, he returned to King's School.

Newton entered Trinity College, Cambridge, in 1661, as a "working" student, meaning he had not enough money of his own to see him through. In 1665 he was awarded his bachelor's degree. Because of the severity of the plague which raged in London in 1665, he returned to Woolsthorpe for a period of eighteen months, a period so important that it must be given special attention. He returned to Cambridge in the latter part of 1666, and two years later was awarded the master's degree. The next year he was appointed as Lucasian Professor of Mathematics at Cambridge, a position his major professor, Isaac Barrow, had not only recommended him for, but had resigned in favor of Newton. Newton delivered his lectures on optics from 1670 to 1672, based on his own early work and on Barrow's. His first paper on optics was published in 1672.

Newton's first major work, the *Principia*, appeared in 1687, but only because of the efforts of Edmund Halley of comet fame. Halley, who would not have discovered the comet had it not been for the *Principia*, had become aware of some of Newton's important discoveries after visiting Cambridge in 1684. He knew of Newton's explanation of gravity as the force which held the universe together, and he worked diligently on the reluctant Newton to get the latter's ideas in print. In 1672 Newton had joined the Royal Society, and in 1687, when the *Principia* was published by the Royal Society, Samuel Pepys, the great diarist and secretary to the Admiralty, was its president. Because the Royal Society had run out of funds in 1687,

Halley, who did not have a great deal of money himself, undertook the cost of publication. Halley also was helpful in seeing the book through publication and in offering editorial assistance.

By 1689 Newton's fame was such that he was elected to Parliament from Cambridge, serving only a year, because in 1690 Parliament was dissolved. A couple of years later, in 1692, when he was fifty years old, Newton became dangerously ill. It was the period of his life when his depression was the strongest and his conduct most erratic; but he was not, as some claimed, insane.

By 1693 Newton had emerged from his slump sufficiently to take an active interest in scientific concerns once again, but he remained sensitive, bordering at times on the neurotic. It has even been suggested that he never regained his ability to deal with scientific problems after 1693, but the evidence simply does not warrant that conclusion.

Newton had long sought some kind of government appointment, but it was slow in coming, resulting in insulting, whining letters to his friends John Locke and Charles Montagu, accusing them of working against him. The charges were false and completely unwarranted. Both men had been good friends of Newton's and remained so all their lives.

Montagu, who was Chancellor of the Exchequer, was instrumental in having Newton appointed as Warden of the Mint in 1696, necessitating Newton's move to London for almost the entire remainder of his life. It was at this juncture that Newton displayed a remarkable ability to carry out administrative responsibilities; and so successful was he in doing so that he would be known as a valuable public figure today even if he had accomplished nothing in science.

As Warden of the Mint, Newton was responsible for overhauling England's coinage system. Coins had been clipped and filed until some of them were only half their face value. All the old coins were called in and replaced with coins of standard weight, shape, and metallic content. Newton's efficiency was such that some who had profited from the defacing of the old coins tried to get Newton fired; and when that failed, they tried to bribe him. That also failed. Newton pursued the "criminals of the coin" with such vigor that many of them ended up on the gallows. Hardly the picture we normally have of one of England's greatest scientists.

In 1699, so successful had Newton been in cleaning up England's monetary mess, that he was appointed Master of the Mint, a position that paid exceedingly well but required much less time than that associated with his duties as warden; it was a job that allowed him time to continue his work on his *Opticks*. But also in that year, 1699, Newton was appointed as a foreign associate of the French Academy of Science, one of only eight to receive so important an honor.

In 1701, when he was fifty-eight, Newton was elected a second time to Parliament, and that same year he resigned the Lucasian Chair in Mathematics which he had held at Cambridge since 1669. Two years later in 1703, he was elected president of the Royal Society, a position which he held until the end of his life.

Newton's second major work, the *Opticks*, was published in England in 1704. Like the *Principia* it was an immediate success, although–also like the *Principia*–it was not without its detractors. Newton was always annoyed by criticism of his work, and was often involved in controversy. A prominent member of the Royal Society, Robert Hooke, an eminent scientist in his own right, locked horns with Newton on several occassions, both with respect to the theory of light and the theory of gravitation. So distasteful was the criticism to Newton that he at one point decided to publish no further accounts of his work. Only the intervention of Halley persuaded him to publish his *Principia* after a delay of twenty-one years; and the *Opticks* had to wait almost forty years–until the year after Hooke's death.

In 1705, Newton was knighted by Queen Anne at Trinity College, becoming the first English scientist to be so honored; and it was not viewed as merely a perfunctory title, as the events at the time of his death would demonstrate. At the time of his knighthood he was recognized as perhaps the leading scientist in all of Europe.

For the last twenty-four years of his life, Newton presided over the weekly meetings of the Royal Society, occasionally falling asleep, but still managing to do what his duties there required.

Although Newton made no great discoveries in the last twenty-two years of his life, his mind remained keen and able to follow second and third editions of the *Principia* and *Opticks* through the press. He managed, moreover, in those years to publish an occasional paper–for example, *On the Nature of Acids*, which appeared in 1710; *De Analysi*, a mathematical work which appeared in 1711; and a book entitled *Universal Arithmetic*, which was put out a few years earlier.

When he was eighty-two, Newton moved to Kensington where he resided for the remaining two years of his life. He died in 1727. His body lay in state before being buried in Westminster Abbey. The famous French philosopher Voltaire traveled from France to attend the funeral. Newton's casket was carried by dukes and earls of the realm–a mark of the great respect in which he was held by the English people.

In searching for the clues to Newton's greatness, one is impressed by the wealth of information that is available. Quite apart from his two major works in science and several lesser works, there exists an astonishing amount of material on subjects relating to the Bible.

The King James Version of the Bible had appeared as recently as 1611, and Newton was an avid student of it all his life. He wrote extensively about matters that interested him in the sphere of religion. It has been suggested by several scholars that one of the reasons for his failure to publish this material is that his religious views were not quite orthodox–particularly in regard to the nature of the Trinity.

He had a great deal to say about the prophecies of Daniel and St. John, and a book containing his views on these subjects came out after his death. A short work dealing with corruptions of the scriptures was published long after his death; but one work, titled the *Chronology of the Ancient Kingdoms Amended*, appeared the year after his death.

In addition to his work on religion and history, he wrote extensively on chemistry and alchemy, none of it apparently intended for publication. But none of this was known even by the scientific public, who knew Newton chiefly by his two stunning publications, the *Principia* and the *Opticks*, the one appearing in Latin in 1687, the other in English in 1704. Had the unpublished material appeared in print–about one and a half million words–it would have filled about twenty-five standard-size volumes.

Now, if one were to pick a time that best expressed Newton's genius, it would be much earlier than the publication dates of his two masterpieces of scientific writing; it would be the years 1665-1666. In English history, 1665-1666 is called the *annus mirabilis*, the Marvelous Year, or the year of wonders; and it took that name from three separate traumatic events which struck London almost simultaneously: The Bubonic Plague, which started late in 1664, and was the worst outbreak since the days of the Black Death in the fourteenth century, had in only two months in the summer of 1665 wiped out one-tenth of the population of London. The Great Fire of London which decimated the older city that same year was credited with stemming the plague, but the city was left in smoldering ruins. As if that were not enough, because England was at war with Holland, the Dutch fleet sailed up the Thames River and threatened London.

By 1665, the plague was so pervasive that Cambridge was closed, and Newton, who had just taken his bachelor's degree, was forced to return to his home in Woolsthorpe. The eighteen months he spent there waiting for Cambridge to reopen were the most eventful months of his life from the perspective of science–his own *annus mirabilis*. During that period, even while he continued his experiments in chemistry and alchemy, often fashioning the materials he needed for his experiments, he worked out the basic laws of mechanics (his three laws of motion), the principle of gravitation, his infinitesimal calculus, and his views on light and color–all this he did while still in his twenties!

Perhaps it was inevitable that someone subscribing to the idea that the entire universe could be described simply as matter in motion, would be compelled to define the laws that governed that motion–assuming it was not all random–or there would be no way of accounting for the mechanical universe. For Newton, then, the laws of motion were a good starting point. The first axiom reads: "Every body perseveres in its state of rest, or of uniform motion in a straight line, unless it is compelled to change that state by impressed forces." The second axiom reads: "Change of motion (i.e. rate of change of momentum) is proportional to the impressed force and takes place in the direction in which that force is impressed." And the third axiom reads: "To every action there is always opposed an equal reaction; or the mutual actions of two bodies upon each other are always equal and opposite."

Actually, the laws of motion were not strictly new. Descartes and Galileo had contributed substantially to the first two, and Newton credits them for doing so. But Newton was the first to state them unequivocally as laws, add the third law, and link the three laws together. Scholars have pointed out contributions to the first two laws by fourteenth century thinkers, antedating both Galileo and Kepler; and they assert that while Newton drew from the experiments of Wallis, Wren, and Huygens for the third law–the only physical law of the three–no one before Newton clearly formulated it. But Leonardo da Vinci had done so a hundred and fifty years earlier, using language almost identical to Newton's.

Although the ideas that Newton so firmly grasped during those fantastically productive eighteen months at Woolsthorpe would not be presented to the world until 1687, practically all of the ideas contained in the *Principia* were born in his home town; they were the product of a mind that penetrated seemingly inscrutable problems until they yielded all their secrets. The laws of motion were the product of experience and observation–his and others. But he took them one step further. With his theory of gravitation, he was careful not to assign the *cause* of motion. He did not presume to know it. But there were a few things he did know with all the certainty of his splendidly intuitive mind, supported by the mathematical formula he had invented to explain it.

The story of the apple falling at his feet may be a myth, but he may well have wondered if the force that attracts the apple to the earth reaches out to attract the moon, and if that force is what keeps the moon in its orbit. Some force was necessary to keep a circular body in orbit, a centripetal force, he reasoned, or, like the apple, it would fall to earth. So, the force that kept the moon circling the earth must be the same force that keeps the earth in its orbit about the sun. All matter in motion was affected by that force. But centripetal is not one force and gravity another. They are the same force.

The speeds that planets traveled in their orbits, Newton calculated, was a function of their distance from the sun; as their distances increased, their speeds decreased. Then he supplied the law he had learned from Kepler while a student at Cambridge: force, like speed, must decrease with distance. The law is known as the "inverse square law." It requires that a planet twice as far away would register a force one quarter as great; a planet three times as far would register a force one ninth as great, etc.

Newton registers his discovery in a manuscript which helps to establish the importance of his *annus mirabilis*: "And the same year [1666] I began to think of gravity extending to the Orb of the Moon, and having found out how to estimate the force with which [a] globe revolving within a sphere presses the surface of the sphere from Kepler's Rule of the periodical times of the Planets being in a sesquialterate proportion of their distances from the centres of their Orbs I deduced that the forces which keep the Planets in their Orbs must [be] reciprocally as the squares of their distances from the centres about which they revolve; and thereby compared the force requisite to keep the Moon in her Orb with the force of gravity at the surface of the Earth, and found them answer pretty nearly."

But, when Newton derived from this his law of universal gravitation, he, like his contemporaries, believed that all orbits of celestial bodies were circular. He was soon to discover that the required orbit under an inverse square law is an ellipse.

When the *Principia* was published in 1687, it appeared in three books. In the first book, Newton sets forth some stunning conclusions. For example, if the sun exerts a force on the planets, the planets exert an equal force on the sun (from the third law or axiom). The apple pulls as hard on the earth as the earth pulls on the apple; but in this case, just as in the case of the respective pull of the sun and its planets, the mass is significantly greater in one body than in the other.

Newton goes on to explain that gravity acts as if all the mass were at the center of the sphere, yet he was to discover that inside the sphere the rule does not apply. As the center is approached, gravity decreases; at the center, gravity is zero. The force of gravity from the outer parts of the sphere cancel each other.

He goes on to show that pull is based on mass or weight. If the mass is doubled, the pull will be doubled. If the moon were half the mass it is, the pull would be half and the centripetal force would retain the balance between the moon and the earth at the same distance.

In Book II of *Principia*, Newton continues his examination of motion; but while Book I deals with motion through media of no or little resistance, Book II deals with motion through media offering resistance, like air or water. Among his investigations in this connection is his determination of the speed of sound.

Book III is a report of applications of the theories contained in Books I and II. It includes his conclusion regarding the shape of the earth, not a perfect sphere as formerly believed, but bulging at the equator because of its rotation on its axis. Also included is a report on the tides, caused by the joint attraction of the moon and the sun. Newton calculated that high tide should occur three hours later than it did, and attributed the difference to inertia. (It was later found to be caused by friction.)

Also included is a discussion of the precession of the equinoxes, caused by the change in direction of the earth's axis. Pointing in the direction of the North Star, the axis of the earth traces a circle around it, caused by the pull of the sun and the moon on the earth's bulging equator. The rate is only fifty seconds of precession a year, and Newton calculated that it would require 26,000 years to make a complete circle.

Newton also tackled the problem of comets, seen only briefly in the sky, and showed that they were affected by gravity, traveling around the sun in elliptical orbits.

It has been suggested that the *Principia* ended a line of investigation in science—that on the motion of celestial bodies—because, after Newton, the matter was thought to be settled once and for all. On the other hand, he opened a new line of investigation with his work on light and colors. But theories about optics hardly began with Newton. Aristotle had some clear-cut notions about light and color, many of which were wrong.

*I*f there is anything that scientists have learned, it is that, true or not, there is no final word in science. Newton's corpuscular theory of optics fell out of fashion with the ascendancy of the wave theory, but the advent of quantum physics has demonstrated that light is a function of both wave and "corpuscle."

Einstein's theory of relativity, enunciated in 1915, seemed to render Newton's law of universal gravitation obsolete; but while on a theoretical level that may be so, on a practical level, Newton's law is still valid. Newton's law of gravity holds as long as an extremely heavy object is not involved. In explaining why Mercury's orbit did not follow the same elliptical path, the principle of relativity was invoked. The inverse square law does hold except near inordinately heavy objects. Newton's laws of motion hold as long as speeds do not approach the speed of light.

Newton knew nothing about the speed of light, but he made the first important discoveries about the nature of it. What makes Newton's approach to optics different is the magnitude of his experimentation. His interest in optics was prompted by difficulties encountered in the telescopes of his day. Light was distorted at the edge by the lenses, and focusing on one area only distorted other areas. Newton made his own telescope, a small six-inch model, using the principle of reflection which was secured by means of a mirror built into the telescope. Since reflection is defined as a condition where the angle of incidence is equal to the angle of refraction, there was no distortion of the image. And, while the problem with the lenses was solved by later generations, in Newton's time the reflecting telescope was a marked improvement over existing instruments.

The story is told of how he got hold of a glass prism, cut a small slit in his blind to let the sunlight through, and noticed that when the light passed through the prism, the rays were bent (refracted) in different directions, revealing the colors of the "spectrum" (Newton's name). When a second prism was added, the colors remained the same. The red, for example, was passed through the second prism as red, and retained its redness when passed through blue glass and reflected off green paper. Although not all colors were displaced in the spectrum, Newton discovered seven colors, the basic colors of violet, indigo, blue, green, yellow, orange, and red. He believed that in his matter-in-motion world, red was caused by larger atoms (corpuscles), which were bent less easily by the prism; violet, on the other hand, was caused by smaller bodies, which were bent more easily. He discovered, too, that mixing the colors gave white again. Mixing some of them, gave a white-like color. Mixing red and yellow, he found, gave orange; mixing yellow and blue gave green.

Newton's great discovery, then, was that the prism did not change the nature of the light given off by the sun; it simply revealed it as the source of color because color was contained in it.

Like the *Principia*, the *Opticks*, which was published in 1704 and went through three editions in Newton's lifetime, consisted of three books. Book I deals with the reflection and refraction of light, the formation of images, the production of spectra by prisms, the properties of colored light, and the composition and dispersion of white light. Book II deals with the production of colors in interference phenomena, and Book III is a record of experiments in diffraction and includes a list of forty-three "Questions," or queries, covering a whole range of subjects.

When Newton began his systematic investigation of light and colors, he revealed himself to be an experimenter of the first order. While his *Principia* was based on theoretical speculation, his *Opticks* was not. He displayed an unusual capacity as a scientist to be as much at home in experimentation as in theoretical speculation. Because the *Opticks* was written in English, it appealed to a much wider audience than did the *Principia*, which was written in Latin. The *Opticks* is, in fact, extremely readable–a claim that cannot be made about many of the great books of science. But that was not enough to keep it in print for one hundred and fifty years, whereas The *Principia* was republished on a regular basis.

So difficult were the mathematics on which the *Principia* was based that many scientists of the day were unable to understand it, and it had to be popularized by the few mathematicians who understood what Newton was up to. The difficulty was exacerbated by the choice of using, for the *Principia*, old geometrical concepts to express ideas more suited to Newton's calculus–but this he had not shared with the scientific world, and he seemed in no hurry to do so. Benjamin Franklin was a great admirer of the *Opticks*, as was Jefferson, and reread it several times. But Franklin, like others not well trained in mathematics, lacked the knowledge to grasp the explanation of gravitation contained in the *Principia*.

In some ways, Newton was as much a figure of the Renaissance as he was of the Age of Discovery; and like Galileo, who died the year that Newton was born, he owed much to the influences of the Middle Ages. One would perhaps find that easier to understand in Galileo's case than in Newton's; but while Galileo took the best that the science of the Middle Ages had to offer, Newton took the worst. And even though Newton had Robert Boyle's books on chemistry in his library, he also had books on alchemy, a favorite magical bias of the Rosicrucians, a secret brotherhood founded in the early seventeen century who drew heavily from the alchemic lore of the Middle Ages. Although Newton has been called "the last of the magicians," and although occult interests were attractive to him all his life, he was as capable of making nature yield her secrets as any man who ever lived. But to do so he, like Galileo, had ultimately to forsake authority. Newton once said, "Plato is my friend, Aristotle is my friend, but my best friend is truth."

But Newton understood, as well as any person alive, the futility of attempting to master the truth of science. A few years before he died, he revealed his assessment of what he had accomplished: "I do not know what may appear to the world, but to myself I seem to have been only like a boy playing on the seashore, and diverting myself in now and then finding a smoother pebble or a prettier shell than ordinary, while the great ocean of truth lay all undiscovered before me." Elusive as it may be, Newton pursued truth all his life.

Truth, as it turns out, has always been the best friend of science.

EINSTEIN

BY
JERRY
ANDERSON

# Albert Einstein

## 1879-1955

"*It is true that the grasping of truth is not possible without empirical basis. However, the deeper we penetrate and the more extensive and embracing our theories become the less empirical knowledge is needed to determine those theories.*"

By whatever title is bestowed upon him— "the greatest genius of the twentieth century" or "the greatest theoretical physicist who ever lived"—Albert Einstein has become a star in his own firmament. His contributions to man's understanding of the universe are without parallel. He changed forever our notions of time, space, motion, and the structure of the cosmos. It seemed as though, it has been said, he was trying to read the mind of God. By almost any account his achievements in science placed him fifty years ahead of his time. Yet his scientific sights may be said to have been aimed at a single target—the nature of light.

It was not only his scientific genius that made him so popular a figure, but his personal qualities of grace, wit, humility, and distaste for all ostentatiousness as well. While not poor by any means, he lived modestly and good-naturedly among his associates. He spent a great deal of time writing letters and lecturing in several different countries. In quiet moments, he played the violin.

As is so often the case with those who position themselves on the threshold of human history, Einstein's theories failed to win adherents from a large part of the scientific community for many years. Although the special theory of relativity was advanced in 1905 and the general theory in 1916, when Einstein was awarded the Nobel Prize in 1922, it was not for his theories of relativity, as one might expect, but for his theory of the photoelectric effect (the photon theory of light), which was a more respected theory at the time the Nobel Prize was awarded.

His humanitarian efforts met with even less enthusiasm from many quarters, where both his politics and his religion were disparaged. Despite his detractors, he held as steadfastly to his principles as to his theories, and, by 1979, the centennial of his birth, he was the honored subject of the scientific world.

But one hundred years earlier, in 1879, such a brilliant career could hardly have been predicted. He was born in Ulm, Germany, a country which had recently extended opportunities for work and education for its Jews. His parents, both nonobservant Jews, moved when he was only a year old to Munich, and, finally, in 1894 to Milan where his father managed a dynamo-manufacturing plant. Albert's early years of schooling were hardly memorable ones.

While still a student at a secondary school in Milan, Einstein received poor grades in history, geography, and language, and he failed the arts portion of an examination which would have enabled him to attend the Zurich Polytechnic (the Swiss Federal Institute of Technology) to qualify for a diploma in electrical engineering. The following year, 1896, he gained admittance to the Zurich school as a student in math and physics; and four years later, in 1900, having again failed to distinguish himself, he graduated as a secondary school teacher.

In 1902, after two years of unsucessful searching for an academic position, he got a job as engineer in a Swiss patent office in Bern, a position he held until 1909. The greatest advantage in his fortuitous move to Bern was the free time his job gave him for following his own projects, even though he was required to spend eight hours a day in his work space. During his years with the patent office, he wrote several technical papers on theoretical physics. This outpouring of scholarly publications was particularly impressive owing to the fact that during those years, 1902 to 1909, he had little contact with other scientists and almost no library resources.

One of the papers, written in 1905, earned him a Ph.D. degree from the University of Zurich. The second paper gained him a position as lecturer at the University of Bern. By 1909 he was considered the leading scientific thinker of German-speaking Europe. That led to his appointment as an associate professor of physics at the University of Zurich. In 1910, he accepted a chair in the University in Prague; in 1912 he was appointed professor of theoretical physics in the Federal Polytechnic in Zurich. In 1914, just before the outbreak of World War I, he relocated to Berlin, then the world's leading center for theoretical physics, by accepting an appointment to the Royal Prussian Academy and to the Kaiser Wilhelm Institute of Physics in Berlin, a position he would hold until 1933; then he accepted his final position with the Institute for Advanced Study at Princeton University.

Einstein was married twice, first in 1903 to Mileva Maritsch, a Zurich University classmate, by whom he had two sons. Recent evidence reveals that, before their marriage, they also had a daughter, Lieserl, whom they gave up for adoption because of the fear that news of the event might cost Einstein his newly found position in Bern. Einstein was unsuitable as a family man, finding little time to give to his wife and sons. Since physics demanded his complete and continuous attention, upon their arrival in Berlin, he and his wife separated. After their divorce in 1919, he married his cousin, Elsa Einstein. By 1919 Einstein must have realized that he was a candidate for the Nobel Prize, because although it was not awarded until three years later, part of his divorce settlement was that Mileva would receive the money from the prize should he receive it.

Between the years 1902 and 1955, the year of his death, Einstein was heavily involved not only in scientific work of the first order, but in humanitarian concerns prompted by two world wars and the events that connected them; but his voice as a humanitarian carried weight only because he was one of the world's leading scientists.

The thing that launched Einstein's career as a world-famous physicist were four papers he published in 1905. They are among the greatest in the history of physics, and contain the first great work in the foundation of molecular physics. The year was Einstein's *annus mirabilis*, just as 1665-66 was Newton's year of wonders. When Einstein began to stun the world with his publications during the years 1902 to 1909, he had never occupied an important academic position. As a scientist he was an amateur. It appears little short of a miracle that this man, before he was thirty years old, could put forth a new set of laws by which nature was governed that would thereafter change the way the universe was viewed.

*T*he first paper to have stunning consequence was Einstein's paper on statistical mechanics, a field that was being investigated by a number of respected scientists. Einstein insisted that his paper could account for Brownian motion. The 'Brownian Movement' was first called to the attention of the scientific world in 1828 by a Scottish botanist named Robert Brown, who observed that when pollen grains were dispersed in a liquid they exhibited an uninterrupted zigzag or swarming motion. The phenomenon attracted the attention of many scientists for several decades. Einstein produced five papers on the subject between 1905 and 1908. His findings confirmed the atomic theory of motion by showing that the velocity of suspended particles, even though unobservable, was caused by collision of the molecules. What made this pronouncement important was that the existence of molecules was not, in 1905, an undisputed assumption. The paper also made it possible to calculate the size of molecules accurately for the first time.

*T*he second of the papers of 1905 was an examination of Max Planck's work on electromagnetic energy emitted from radiating objects. Planck, in 1900, had found that this energy was directly proportional to the frequency of the radiation; that is, the emission and absorption of radiation by atoms was not continuous, but was emitted in discrete units. Planck called these discrete units of energy 'light quanta.' The result perplexed scientists because electromagnetic theory, based on the laws of thermodynamics, had assumed the presence of an ever-present ether that made it possible for the waves of light to contain any amount of energy. The wave theory did not explain why a beam of light striking a metal object could form an electric current, producing what came to be called the 'photoelectric effect.'

What Einstein was able to show was that these light quanta could consist of discrete bundles of radiation—later called photons—and that the so-called photoelectric effect consisted of certain metals giving off electrons when they were illuminated by light having a certain frequency. While Einstein accepted the wave theory of light, he suggested that light had a corpuscular aspect as well. It is not correct, however, to regard Einstein as the discoverer of the corpuscular theory of light if by corpuscle is meant the photon, because Newton had advanced that theory two hundred years earlier. And while Einstein resorted to statistical methods to

account for particle motion, it was only because the large number of particles prevented an account of their motion by any other means. His discovery was to become the basis for what would be called 'quantum mechanics,' a major work of investigation for physicists which had a significant impact on Einstein's life and work.

In a third and certainly his most famous paper of 1905, Einstein put forth his views on special relativity. When his views became known, the ideas about time and space were changed forever. From H.S. Lorentz's work, Einstein knew that when an electron approached the speed of light, its mass increases; and, from Maxwell, Einstein learned of the velocity of electromagnetic waves. But Einstein discovered that other strange phenomena also occurred. Reflecting upon the problem of kinetic motion, Einstein reformulated the classical principle of relativity which scientists had adhered to since Newton's time—that the laws of physics had to be expressed in the same form regardless of the frame of reference from which they were viewed (though it was impossible to perform any experiment to determine the absolute velocity of any inertial frame). So, the equations used to describe the motion of an electron could also be used to describe the non-accelerated motion of any particle of matter. Einstein assumed, too, following Maxwell's theory, that the speed of light—indeed of all electromagnetic waves—remained a constant 186,000 miles per

second, regardless of the frame of reference. But if the speed of light was constant, something else must vary—time. Time, then, is relative.

What Einstein abandoned in arriving at his new view of relativity was Maxwell's 'ether' because he had no need for it, as Maxwell did. For Maxwell, ether was the medium which carried the electromagnetic waves. It provided a standard against which all motion could be measured, including absolute rest. So, if light was assigned a fixed speed, it had to be relative to something, and Maxwell made it relative to the ether. Nor was ether useful in the interpretation of Lorentz's theory. Einstein did, though, pick up on the theory of time dilation, which makes time, like length and mass, a function of the velocity of discrete frames of reference. Now since the laws of electromagnetism, like all laws of dynamics, must be the same in all frames of reference in uniform relative motion, no absolute velocity can be measured; but its velocity must be the same for all observers in those frames. Put another way, it means that, regardless of their speed, all observers should measure the same speed of light. That is because, in Einstein's theory, all observers are equal—there is no way of knowing which speed is the true speed. Not only that, but steady motion in a straight line is indistinguishable from being at rest (as anyone who has flown in an airplane has discovered).

*T*hus, while Einstein was not the first to assemble the pieces needed to describe the theory of special relativity, he was the first to make the pieces yield a coherent picture. But to do so he had to abandon the Newtonian concept of time as absolute. Only events that occur in our immediate area of the universe can be simultaneous, he argued. For events far removed, its time of occurrence can be arrived at only by knowing its distance and the velocity of light. Stephen Hawking, the Cambridge University Cosmologist, employs an interesting illustration of this: If the sun were suddenly to cease to shine, nothing on earth would reveal that event simultaneously. Since it takes eight minutes for the light of the sun to reach the earth, we could not know about the sun's light going out before eight minutes had passed. Then again, light from distant galaxies takes millions of years to get to us; and since light from the farthest object visible in the sky left its source some eight thousand

million years ago, all we see when looking at it is its ancient past.

What becomes apparent in all this is that absolute time has been abandoned, just as absolute position in space had to be abandoned in Newton's gravitational theory. But the special theory of relativity had to wait forty years to be confirmed.

But what does it mean to say that we live in a relativistic universe? It means that matter must be in motion at very high speeds. When acceleration is significantly increased, a series of remarkable events takes place: time slows down, mass increases, and length decreases. These phenomena would occur at both the microscopic and cosmological levels of physical reality. All this takes place at about ten percent of the speed of light. In Einstein's theory the speed of light acts as a limiting velocity: it represents the fastest speed that information can be processed. From a practical standpoint (as well as a theoretical one) no moving body could attain it, because at the speed of light, length shrinks to zero, and time stands still.

Now, if all physical, chemical, and biological processes slow down when reaching relativistic speeds, there should be some way of confirming it, and the invention of the particle accelerator permitted just that. When particles have been accelerated to high velocities and then made to collide with other particles, disintegration takes place at known rates. But when even higher velocities are attained, disintegration of particles takes place more slowly, in exact agreement with Einstein's predictions.

Several fascinating scenarios have been established to demonstrate the dramatic effects of time dilation, the most popular of which has been called the 'twin paradox'—a paradox for those who believe in absolute time. An abbreviated account goes something like this: Two twins are twenty years old. One becomes an astronaut and travels to a planet which orbits the star Rigil Kent, about four light years away. He travels at 148,000 miles per second, which is 4/5 the speed of light. The clocks on his spaceship would measure 3/5 of the time measured by that of his twin's clock back on earth. So he would make the trip to Rigil Kent in six years—three out and three back. But, while he was gone, his brother on earth would have aged ten years. He measured his twin's travel time as five years out and five years back. Both measurements are correct! One brother would have aged six years, the other ten. The lesson? Time is relative.

The increase in mass at relativistic speeds is shown by the need to adjust the strength of magnetic fields of particle acceleration in order to keep the particles contained within the magnetic field. While decrease in length has not yet been established, physicists see no need to doubt its occurrence.

In a short fourth paper of 1905, a post-script to his paper on relativity, Einstein explained the mathematical support for his special theory of relativity. It was the disarmingly simple formula: $E = mc^2$. In other words, mass (m), multiplied by the speed of light (c) squared, is equal to energy (e). As Nigel Calder points out, prior to Einstein's stunning intuitive insight into their equivalency, mass and energy were considered as two distinct things. And, more than that, the value of the energy of a body at rest could be arbitrarily assigned.

What special relativity implies is that the energy of a body at rest is $mc^2$. Put another way, each physical body of mass has an $mc^2$ of rest energy which can be converted to other kinds of energy. But this means that in converting its rest energy the body loses part of its mass. Although this happens in all chemical reactions—the sun being perhaps the most obvious—the significance of this for nuclear reactions is well known.

Einstein became increasingly interested in extending the special theory in relativity to bodies with accelerated motion. In 1907 he introduced the principle of equivalence which held that there was no difference between gravitational acceleration and that caused by mechanical force. Gravitational mass was, in other words, the same as inertial mass.

But Einstein needed to bring both gravitational and electromagnetic acceleration under a single physical formula, rather than simply reduce optics to mechanics. So, in his 1907 paper, he postulated that if mass and energy were equal, then this principle of equivalence would suggest that gravitational mass would interact with an appropriate mass of electromagnetic radiation, which includes light. By 1911 he was able to predict that a ray of light from a distant star, passing near the sun, would appear to be bent slightly in the direction of the sun, producing a slight variation between the star's real and apparent position. Einstein's theory of general relativity was published in 1916, after he had settled in Berlin, and his prediction about bent light in a gravitational field was verified in 1919 by two British expeditions during a solar-eclipse. The confirmation of his theory made him instantly world-famous.

In the special theory of relativity, Einstein restricted its application to observers in uniform relative motion. This was in keeping with the Newtonian theory of the difference between uniform and accelerated motion. But such motions could be understood only in terms of absolute space. So Einstein's general theory of relativity was an extension of relativity to apply to observers in all types of relative motion. He argued that the laws of nature should be stated in a way that would apply to any designated space and time coordinates. Now since accelerated motion could  be distinguished from uniform motion only by the action of force, Einstein wished to eliminate it from consideration; and in the case of gravity, he was successful, by reducing it to a geometrical theory. This, it is said, is the outstanding achievement of the general theory.

In this regard—as in so many other instances—Einstein received inspiration from other scientists, including the mathematicians Herman Minkowski and Bernhard Riemann, who provided Einstein with a mathematical model for his theory. Einstein knew, as did others, that in a local environment, where motion can be regarded as uniform, all falling bodies have the same acceleration; and so, relative to each other, their motion could be said to be unaccelerated. Thus motion in a gravitational field is equivalent to uniform motion.

It was the theory of general relativity that caught the attention of the scientific world, and that was because it presented a wholly new account of gravity. Prior to Einstein, gravity was based on the theory of Newton, whose 1687 law of universal gravitation held that gravity was a force that is exerted on all objects in the universe, attracting them to each other, and that the same force that links the earth and an apple, links the earth and a distant star.

But Einstein believed that Newton was wrong about gravity, suggesting that it is a field, much like a magnetic field, and that matter and energy create the gravitational field by distorting the space around it. Because the space is distorted, or curved, the shortest distance between two points need no longer be thought of as a straight line. Though the earth and other satellites appear to move in circular orbits in three-dimensional space in keeping with Newton's theory, they do not. They follow the shortest path possible in curved space, a path that is called a 'geodesic.' It was the curved-space concept that was tested by the British expeditions. When the star appeared in the darkness of the eclipse to be farther from the solar disk than normal, the light must be bent by the sun's gravitational field. No other explanation seemed possible. But Einstein's general theory of relativity seemed applicable only at the cosmological level. His theory retained the elements of the 'classical theory' because he left electromagnetism out of the equation (just as he had left gravity out of the special theory), thereby not taking into account principles of relativity.

Science accepted the axiom that laws of physics are capable of being mathematically expressed. Because they are not related to time, place, or circumstance, the laws are invariable, and not dependent upon observation. For Einstein, this remained an important caveat. In his relativistic universe, laws applicable to one frame of reference applied to all frames of reference, even though the effects of those laws differed.

Although Einstein employed his intuition in a manner that freed him from the rigid requirements of classical physics, he remained convinced that truth was independent of man. The question for science always remained the same. Do the theories produced by the human mind correspond to the objective world of nature? Because Einstein believed that the universe is governed by immutable laws, and is therefore rational, human reason was capable of providing a synthesis for all the disparate elements of nature.

This belief presented Einstein with unresolvable problems in two related areas—in quantum mechanics and in the 'unified field' theory. Einstein's contributions to quantum mechanics were significant. His paper on the photoelectric effect of light helped to prepare the way for the quantum theory. But the theory would produce conclusions that Einstein could not accept—that nature is somehow subjective and that the observer cannot be separated from what is observed. This became known as the 'uncertainty principle.' It has been suggested that Einstein confused uncertainty in its subatomic, statistical sense with uncertainty about cause and effect, and the fact that the effect of this made man more a part of nature, less alienated, was of no concern to Einstein.

*T*he 'uncertainty principle' of quantum mechanics stipulates that the very act of observing subatomic particles disturbs their state so that precise measurements of the motion and position of particles cannot be obtained. Now since all empirical knowledge is hypothetical and probable at best, no knowledge provided by the senses is certain. But scientists working with submicroscopic entities never see particles in motion, only traces left by the interaction of particles on photographic plates.

It is not that matter itself presented that much of a mystery. All material in the universe was said to be made up of molecules, and the molecules themselves were made up of a relatively few number of atoms, of which a hundred or so have been identified, beginning with hydrogen, the lightest, and extending to the heavy uranium atom and beyond. But all molecules—which means all matter in the universe—are made up of these hundred or so known atoms, which became familiarly expressed in the Periodic Table of Elements. And each of these limited number of atoms is composed of only three basic particles—protons, neutrons, and electrons. It was Einstein's insistence that elementary particles were governed by rigid laws of causality that was to separate him from the mainstream of scientific inquiry in the last thirty years of his life.

While Einstein subscribed to the idea that scientists should follow the evidence wherever it leads, where quantum science was concerned, he believed that the conclusions should be regarded merely as tentative, and that they were, in fact, misleading. But on this score Einstein was wrong. The evidence supporting the "uncertainty principle" was too apparent to be ignored. Einstein was aware that since the ancient Greeks, reality of nature was to be discovered by looking into the fundamental units of matter, and he admitted that the quantum theory had been successful in explaining many problems associated with atoms and subatomic particles.

Scientists had found that quanta can be described only as collections of particles. Individual particles did not adhere to the precise law of cause and effect as required by classical mechanics, meaning that their precise measurement is not possible. Their motion and position can be measured only in statistical terms.

Now it can be argued that if the measurement of fundamental particles is inexact, and that reason demands the exact measurement of the elements of nature, then the universe is irrational. Einstein could not accept such a conclusion. He clung always to his belief in an ordered universe created by a God who wouldn't let individual particles slip through the cracks of His magnificent creation. Well known is his remark, "I can't believe that God plays dice with the universe." Less known is Niel Bohr's response, "Stop telling God what to do." But then Einstein could never accept Bohr's view that the universe is neither causal nor deterministic. He clung to his belief in physical reality as a four-dimensional space-time continuum, with events already determined.

*E*instein was unable to link the four known forces of nature into a unified field theory, and his 1950 attempt was as coolly received as his 1929 effort. Since the quantum theory holds that all motion is ultimately unstable, how could he be expected to succeed? His fear was that if he did not do it, no one would.

The four known forces may be described as those that cause motion. One form is gravity, which is generally described by the inverse-square law. Its cause is as much a mystery to molecular scientists as it was to Newton. It is the least understood force in terms of its effect—making the orbits of satellites possible. It seems to be the only force that is irreversible—that is, it pulls, but never pushes—and it is the feeblest of the four forces.

A second force, the electromagnetic, affects only electrically charged particles. It accounts for the action of magnets on iron, the combining of atoms into molecules, and even for signals received by the brain. Both the gravitational and the electromagnetic forms are found in great mass at the cosmo-

logical level, but the last two—the strong and weak nuclear forces—are found at the sub-atomic level. The electromagnetic force is between the strong and weak nuclear forces in strength.

The strong force binds the nucleus of the atom. The nucleus is made up of protons which are positively charged and of neutrons which have no charge. They should repel each other, but they do not because of the presence of an exceptionally strong force which overcomes the electromagnetic repulsion. This strong nuclear force, which can bind hundreds of protons and neutrons into a single nucleus is the force which causes the reaction which powers the stars and the hydrogen bomb. It is one thousand trillion, trillion, trillion times as powerful as  gravity, yet it works only between particles separated by one trillionth of an inch.

The fourth known force that causes motion is called the weak interaction. It works only with specific sub-atomic particles and always works to bring about their disintegration. This weak nuclear force is only one-hundred thousandth as powerful as the strong force, but it is responsible for part of the radioactivity from nuclear wastes and for some of the energy of the stars.

It has for some time been clear that these are not the only forces operating in nature, and scientists since Einstein's time have come up with such names for other subatomic particles as 'quarks,' and 'gluons,' and 'pions,' and 'mu-mesons' or 'muons'; but of these Einstein was unfamiliar. He could not, however, divorce himself from his belief in a universe that revealed itself by means of precise mathematical laws; and thirty years of his life were spent in a futile search for an equation which would link these known forces into a single formula or equation—into a unified field theory. His chances for success were seemingly impossible because of the discovery of the uncertainty principle in all measurements of the motion of particles.

But what if the laws of reality are the laws of human nature? Can self-conscious observation be divorced from the structure of human thought? It is the inseparability of the observer from the observed which supports the conclusions of the quantum theory. Now the relativity theory asserted that laws applicable to one frame of reference must be applicable to all frames of reference. But the uncertainty principle of the quantum theory changed all that. The very act of observing sub-atomic particles distorts their state; so one cannot obtain precise measurements of particle positions and particle motions. Measurements are thus dependent upon the observer.

Einstein could never accept such a preposterous notion. So profound was Einstein's belief in the order of the universe that he was forced to find a means of accounting for its apparent disorder. He had, in other words, to make a static universe out of a seemingly dynamic one. Since space-time had a tendency to contract under the gravity theory, he introduced an anti-gravity force which would exactly offset the effect of gravity. But this 'cosmological constant,' as it was called, was introduced for the wrong reason–to satisfy a personal prejudice–, and he later called introducing it the biggest mistake of his life.

Still, Einstein could not fail to recognize that there was a problem. In a relativistic universe–meaning there is no privileged frame of reference–, there are certain social and political as well as scientific ramifications. If there is no privileged frame of reference, is there any point of view–scientific, social, political, or religious–by virtue of which all other points of view are made incorrect?

It thus became easy to apply relativism to all human experience. In what consciously conceived area of human experience, it was asked, is the observer not a participant? But the argument was carried too far. Ethical subjection, for example, can hardly be likened to subjectivity in science, and it was a colossal error to think it could be.

The use of the name 'relativity' proved to be an unfortunate choice. Nigel Calder calls it a "thoroughly bad name" for the theory, and he points out that Einstein considered calling the special theory an "invariance

theory." Still, Calder suggests that the chief merit in the use of the name 'relativity' is that it calls attention to the fact that "the scientist is unavoidably a participant in the system he is studying," and that Einstein "gave the observer his proper status in modern science."

While Einstein was working out his theory of general relativity, World War I was about to break out in Europe. In spite of the hostile feeling against him because he was a Jew and an ardent pacifist, Einstein became a German citizen. (He had become a Swiss citizen after his graduation from the Zurich Polytechnic.) His great reputation did not prevent him from being enmeshed in controversy from 1905 until 1917. In the latter year he published his first version of his 'unified field' theory, which was coolly received by the scientific community; and in that same year he collapsed near death, and was nursed back to health by Elsa.

In the early 30's he spent winters as a visiting professor at the Californian Institute of Technology. When Hitler came to power in 1933, Einstein was abroad. He never returned to Germany, although he got as far as Belgium, where he was assigned bodyguards by King Albert until he could be put on a boat to the United States. He was offered a position as professor of mathematics in the newly created Institute for Advanced Study at Princeton, a position he held for the remainder of his life.

When the Nazi storm troopers ransacked his summer home near Berlin and confiscated his beloved sailboat, Einstein renounced his German citizenship and made an abrupt change in his attitude about peace. He began to urge the allied countries to arm for defense. In 1939, convinced by Leo Szeilard, Eugene Wigner, and Edward Teller, all immigrants and scientists, Einstein wrote a letter to President Franklin D. Roosevelt, urging him to take special notice of the work being done by Berlin scientists in their attempt to build an atomic bomb. The letter is said to have marked the beginning of the Manhattan Project. Almost immediately after the development of the atomic bomb by the United States, Einstein again took up the cause of peace, warning against the effects of uncontrolled use of atomic power. He became an even stauncher supporter of world government, believing that the atomic age was a strong argument for world law. "Nationalism," he wrote, "is an infantile sickness. It is the measles of the human race."

The events of the early 30's changed Einstein. He was disgusted with the failure of the League of Nations to take any meaningful action after World War I to bring about a lasting peace. He resigned from the Committee on Intellectual Cooperation on which his friend Marie Curie also served; and he promoted movements in his name to work for peace, such as the War Resisters International Fund, organized to put pressure on the World Disarmament Committee.

In his religion, Einstein is best described as a moderate. He did not believe in a personal God, but in the God of Spinoza (a seventeenth century Jew), who revealed himself through his creation. The year before his death, in 1954, he wrote, "If something is in me which can be called religious then it is the unbounded admiration for the structure of the world so far as our science can reveal it." The universe, he believed, was the result of neither chance nor chaos.

His support of the Zionist movement was substantial. He was alarmed by the anti-Jewish sentiment spreading across Europe. He was a friend of Chaim Weizman, the first president of Israel. In 1952 Einstein declined an invitation by Ben Gurion to be Israel's new president, saying that politics is a passing thing, but science will be with us forever.

Einstein's writings contain several references to man's moral and religious life, but not because he believed that his being a scientist gave him any special moral insight. The humanitarian impulses he so abundantly possessed were forever being expressed in one form or another. Typical is his observation, "In the last analysis, everyone is a human being, irrespective of whether he is an American or a German, a Jew or a Gentile. If it were possible to manage with this point of view, which is the only dignified one, I would be a happy man. I find it very sad that divisions according to citizenship and cultural tradition should play so great a role in modern practical life. But since this cannot be changed, one should not close one's eyes to reality."

The death of his wife almost twenty years before his own death produced no significant change in Einstein. Alone, largely neglected by the scientific community, he continued to find pleasure in his violin. Most importantly

perhaps, he was at peace with himself. In March 1955, a few weeks before his death, he wrote to Kurt Blunenfeld, the man who had introduced him to Zionism saying, "I thank you, even at this late hour, for having helped me become aware of my Jewish soul."

Not the least of Einstein's accomplishments was his contribution to the philosophy of science, about which he had a great deal to say. For philosophy, itself, he had a tremendous respect. "Philosophy is like a mother," he said, "who gave birth to and endowed all the other sciences. Therefore one should not scorn her in her nakedness and poverty, but should hope, rather, that part of her Don Quixote ideal will live on in her children so that they do not sink into philistinism."

In his attempt to answer the question of the "purpose for the life of the individual and of mankind as a whole," Einstein, in one of his letters, reflectively asserts, "...We all feel that it is indeed very reasonable and important to ask ourselves how we should try to conduct our lives. The answer is, in my opinion: satisfaction of the desires and needs of all, as far as this can be achieved, and achievement of harmony and beauty in the human relationships. This presupposes a good deal of conscious thought and of self-education. It is undeniable that the enlightened Greeks and the old Oriental sages had achieved a higher level in this all-important field than what is alive in our schools and universities." For Einstein, submerging the interest of individuals and communities to the interest of mankind as a whole seemed always the right course of action.

Remarkable revelations from science will continue to startle and thrill us. Still, Einstein's niche in intellectual history seems secure. Nigel Calder sums it up this way: "Einstein's achievement will stand. Some of his premises and prejudices will no doubt be relegated as historical curiosities, when they are either contradicted or superseded by a greater edifice. But nothing will ever eradicate the accomplishments of 1905-17. Then, like a child playing with so many shining beads, he strung together matter and energy and space and time, fashioning from them a girdle for the universe. Even in our cynical century we can safely speak of the young Einstein in the words that the physicist Edmund Halley composed for his friend Isaac Newton:

'Nearer the gods no mortal may approach'."

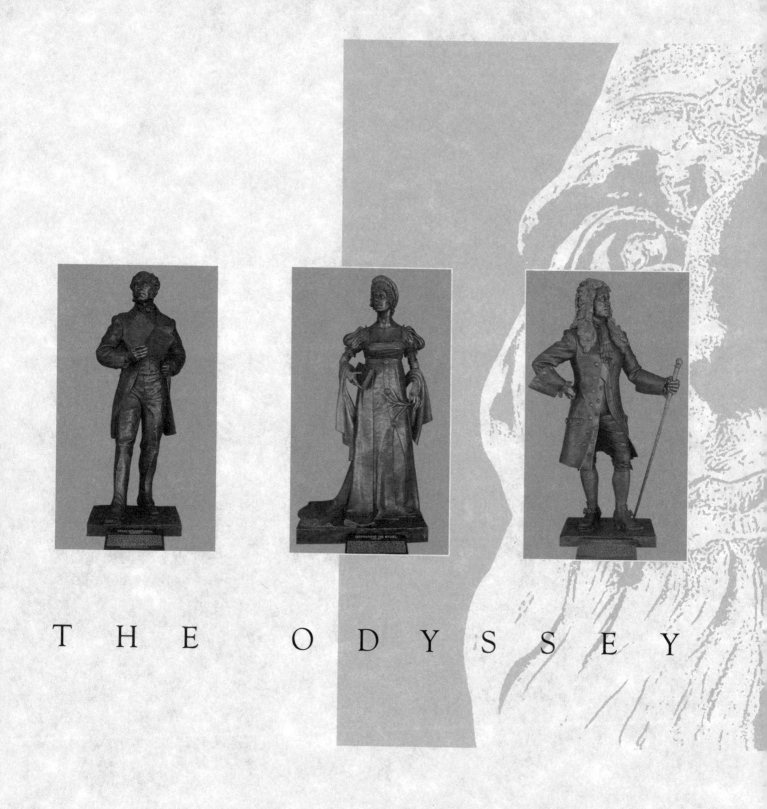

THE ODYSSEY